TABLE OF CONTENTS

LIST OF FIGURES

INTRODUCTION

The United States continues to wrestle with the strategy and execution of its wars in Iraq and Afghanistan. What many initially thought would be relatively simple victories in those countries have become long and drawn out engagements with increasingly blurred policy, strategy, and definitions of victory. Both wars mark a significant shift in complexity from the previous century of interstate conflict bounded by the major conflagrations of World Wars I and II, and the smoldering, latent competition of the Cold War. The shift in complexity and the lengthy search for an elusive victory in both conflicts has given way to disagreements between military and civilian leaders as to the way forward.

In order to be effective in the future strategic environment, U.S. civilian and military leaders will need to better harmonize relationships and efforts. In the recent aftermath of Secretary of Defense Gates' dismissal of several senior military and civilian leaders, and with the recent firing of Army General Stanley McChrystal following a revealing article in *Rolling Stone*, it is clear there is still much work to be done to harmonize efforts and limit the friction generated within the critical civil-military relationship. U.S. engagement in the future strategic environment will undoubtedly demand better coordination if the U.S. is to bring its still formidable resources to bear on the complex challenges of the future.

The historical record, as well as recent events, indicate that current and future American senior military leaders could certainly benefit from a deeper understanding of U.S. civil-military relations. With the Joint Advanced Warfighting School (JAWS)

1

focused on educating rising senior military leaders on the art of translating high-level strategy into operational ways and means, the addition of a civil-military relations course to the curriculum will better prepare rising military leaders to better leverage the civil-military relationship and enhance the level of collaboration demanded by the nation's future strategic challenges. To that end, this thesis offers both a suggested Joint Advanced Warfighting School (JAWS) curriculum and an annotated bibliography of sources on civil-military relations for others to use as appropriate.

To establish a foundation of knowledge upon which to build that understanding, one should begin with conceptual appreciation for the "founding fathers" of U.S. civil-military relations theory--Samuel Huntington and Morris Janowitz, as well as a working knowledge of more contemporary theorists and commentators such as Peter Feaver and Richard Kohn. Theories, however, are mere words unless they can explain past actions and inform future decisions. As such, the emerging senior military leader must also understand the evolution of civil-military relations, particularly as it has evolved since the end of World War II. Of specific interest are the civil-military conflicts that occurred during the Korean, Vietnam, and Afghanistan/Iraq wars and their impact on U.S. war aims and execution. Finally, future senior leaders armed with an appreciation of civil-military theory and conversant in its application, have two additional responsibilities. First, they must continue to read and study issues surrounding the core challenge of their profession. Second, they must educate subsequent generations of officers so as to avoid repeating past mistakes.

Chapter One introduces and summarizes three touchstone civil-military relations theories. These theories developed following World War II and form the foundation of

U.S. civil-military relations today. Chapter Two offers case studies of the Korean and Vietnam wars and the on-going operations in Iraq and Afghanistan, highlighting critical disconnects between civilian policy makers and warfighting military leaders. Drawing upon these theories and case studies, Chapter Three frames the issue and provides questions for further thought. Finally, Chapter Four concludes and proposes a potential civil-military relations course for use in the JAWS curriculum.

CHAPTER 1: NOTABLE CIVIL-MILITARY THEORISTS

Samuel Huntington – Institutional Theory

Published in 1957, Samuel Huntington's *The Soldier and the State* was the first notable attempt to define and describe the phenomena of U.S. civil-military relations. Huntington, a Harvard professor of political science, intended his work to, "…suggest a more useful and relevant framework and to raise and define the principle theoretical issues involved in the study of civil-military relations." As Huntington stated, "Its most important purpose will be served if it stimulates further thinking about civil-military relations and national security." He was inspired to write on the subject due to the lack of theoretical study surrounding civil-military relations, with the only existing theories being "…a confused and unsystematic set of assumptions and beliefs derived from the underlying premises of American liberalism."[1] Huntington acknowledged his theory on civil-military relations (like any theory), may not completely capture all of the elements and facts and their interaction, but should serve as a starting point for how to look at and relate to the phenomena. He acknowledged that any theory requires abstraction, and in some cases over-simplification of the elements, in order to be able to place them into categories from which to work.[2] He conceded that the real world "is one of blends, irrationalities and incongruities…with actual personalities, institutions, and beliefs that do not fit into neat logical categories."[3] However, having a broad understanding and applying his theoretical framework in the dynamic context of the "real world" will

---

[1] Samuel Huntington, *The Soldier and the State: The Theory and Politics of Civil-Military Relations* (New York: Vintage Books, 1957), vii-viii.
[2] Ibid.
[3] Ibid.

perhaps leave one with a better understanding and clarification of the civil-military

relationship and be able to apply its "…lessons for broader application and use."[4]

Huntington's work on the study of civil-military relations is expansive. Given the

focus of this paper, the most applicable portion is the first section of *The Soldier and the

State*, which deals primarily with officership and the military profession as it relates to

the civil-military relationship and the formulation of policy and the military operations

that carry it out. It is here that he delivers the basis of his theory, describing what he sees

as the factors that influence the military and their interplay with the American society and

its civilian leaders.

Huntington proposes there are two imperatives that influence and shape the

military in any society. The first being the "functional imperative" of the military's

mission to protect and provide security from potential external threats. The second

"societal imperative" stems from a military force drawn from and manned by the very

society it protects and serves, and therefore, influenced and shaped by the ideologies,

values, and sentiment dominant within that society.[5] It is upon the relationship between

these two "imperatives" that Huntington centers much of his civil-military relational

model--to defend the nation while simultaneously drawing manpower from it and being

shaped by its evolving norms. Huntington further separates the societal imperative into

two components, "ideology" and "structure." "Ideology" describes the "ebb and flow" of

American society's political views and stance over time (ranging from pro-military to

anti-military), while "structure" refers to the rules and regulations that provide guidance

---

[4] Ibid., vii.
[5] Ibid., 2.

at the institutional level and serve as a framework from which the civil-military relationship is born.[6]

The "functional imperative" of a nation's requirement to field a military in order to thwart outside threats and the "societal imperative" of the collective views of society and how it relates to the use of that force, are what Huntington refers to as "independent variables" that define the nature of the military institution and are "the nub of the problem of civil-military relations."[7] As dynamic as these two variables may seem, Huntington viewed them as "constants" that would always be relevant factors in the civil-military relationship. "Huntington's imperatives are the independent variables that explain changes in the dependent variable of civilian control, which itself becomes an explanatory variable to predict changes in the level of military security."[8] In other words, Huntington argued that the level of military security a nation produced would be the product of how well the civilian control of the military balanced and managed the "functional" and "societal" imperatives.

Huntington points out that while the societal imperative (ideology and structure) remains a relative constant in the civil-military relationship over time, the one major variable driving friction within this relationship (and perhaps explaining its effectiveness or lack thereof) is the functional imperative of the external threat. Huntington argued that with a very low external threat to the nation, overall security of the nation is not at stake and is taken for granted. Therefore, issues concerning civil-military relations are turned more "inward" and deal more with internal issues which are "limited to the impact of the

---

[6] Feaver, Peter D., "The Civil-Military Problematique: Huntington, Janowitz and the Question of Civilan Control," *Armed Forces & Society* (Winter 1996): 155-161.
[7] Huntington, *The Soldier and the State*, 2.
[8] Feaver, "The Civil-Military Problematique," 7.

military institutions upon domestic, economic and political values and institutions."[9]

Within the context of the 1960s and the developing Cold War with the Soviet Union,

Huntington argued that given increases in technology and the U.S.'s increased global

political role, security would now become "…the final goal rather than its starting

assumption."[10] He felt previous era's civil-military relations issues centered around

military compatibility with American values (e.g., ideals about the "citizen-soldier"), and

that the (then) present-day threat of a nuclear armed Soviet Union, which he viewed as a

long-standing and permanent threat to the U.S., would now drive the more important

debate over the pattern of civil-military relations most appropriate to maintain American

security.[11] Huntington viewed the policy and strategy of an ever-increasing and

expansive military force to counter the increasing Soviet threat to be at odds with

society's long-standing liberal ideology, which he thought would infringe on and hamper

the military's "expertise" in doing its job and providing for the security of the nation.

Huntington's solution to this dilemma was to return to the "dependent variable" of

civilian control. Huntington proposed the system best suited to maximize military

security without losing the effectiveness and supremacy of civilian control was through a

system of "objective control, " which he argued most effectively led to the maximization

of "military professionalism" and security of the state.[12]

As Huntington put it, "Civilian control in the objective sense is the maximization

of military professionalism. More precisely, it is that distribution of political power

between the military and civilian groups which is most conductive to the emergence of

---

[9] Huntington, *The Soldier and the State*, 2.
[10] Ibid., 3.
[11] Ibid.
[12] Ibid., 83.

processional attitudes and behavior among the members of the officer corps."[13] In short, Huntington argued that in order to maximize military effectiveness, efficiency and professionalism, the military must operate in its own separate sphere of expertise, detached and not involved with the politics and policy that enable its application, where any "…interference or meddling in military affairs undermines military professionalism and so undermines objective control."[14] Under objective control, "professional" military officers serve at the pleasure of the state, are "politically sterile and neutral," and would not be subject to the societal imperatives that Huntington argued threatened national security.[15] As Peter Feaver, a professor of political science at Duke University and author of several books and articles on civil-military relations puts it, "Huntington's causal chain is as follows: autonomy leads to professionalization, which leads to political neutrality and voluntary subordination, which leads to secure civilian control."[16] Huntington argued that by professionalizing the military in this way, the military's political influence is minimized with respect to civilian control, but maximized with respect to its ability (and morale) to operate effectively and project power (illustrated in Figure 1).[17]

---

[13] Huntington, *The Soldier and the State*, 83.

[14] Feaver, "The Civil-Military Problematique," 160.

[15] Huntington, *The Soldier and the State*, 83-84; Peter D. Feaver and Richard H. Kohn, *Soldiers and Civilians: The Civil-Military Gap and American National Security* (Cambridge, Massachusetts: MIT Press, 2001), 5.

[16] Feaver, "The Civil-Military Problematique," 160.

[17] Huntington, *The Soldier and the State*, 84.

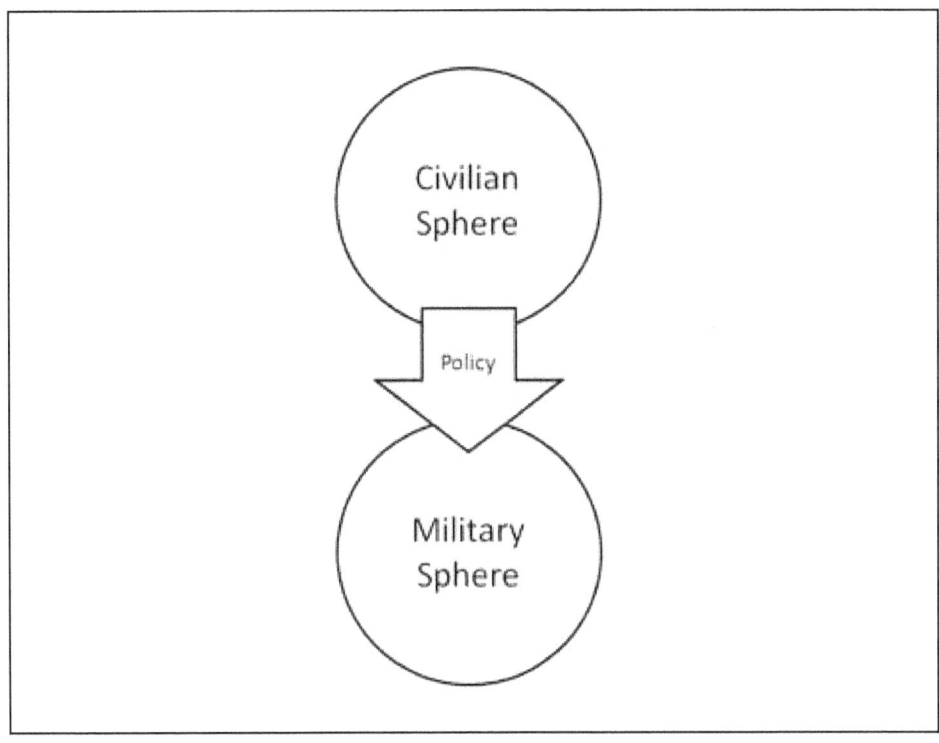

Figure 1. Huntington's Objective Control[18]

The opposite of objective control is what Huntington referred to as "subjective

control," which he argued America should avoid, as it would result in a military force

unable to meet the needs of the long-term threat. Under subjective control, a separate and

independent military does not exist. Civilian control of the military occurs by ensuring

the military force more closely resembles and mimics the civilian society (civilianizing)

until it becomes a "mirror of the state."[19] Huntington argued that objective and

subjective control are inversely proportional with relation to civilian control. Increases in

subjective control would actually reduce the ability of civilian leaders to control military

actions. The more the military becomes involved in the politics and institutional affairs

---

[18] Alexus G Grynkewich, "The Airman and the State: An F-22 Pilot's Perspective on Civil-Military Relations" (Masters Thesis, Joint Advanced Warfighting School, 2010), 6.

[19] Huntington, *The Soldier and the State*, 83.

of national security, the more its overall military effectiveness suffers and it is less able to protect the state.

Huntington points out, "Historically, the demand for objective control has come from the military profession, the demand for subjective control from the multifarious civilian groups anxious to maximize their power in military affairs."[20] Contrary to the idea of subjective control, objective control then *minimizes* and limits the influential power of the military relative to that of civilian control, thereby minimizing any potential inherent political power it may exercise over its civilian counterparts. In doing this, objective control "preserves that essential element of power which is necessary for the existence of the military profession." It is this system of objective control that Huntington believed maximized military professionalism, and thereby maximized the effectiveness of the military, drawing its power from the "legitimate authority within the state."[21]

One of the key factors in Huntington's concept (which he refers to as the fundamental thesis) of objective control is professionalism and the idea of officership as a "profession." Huntington defines a profession as "a functional group with highly specialized characteristics"--specifically, expertise, responsibility and corporateness.[22] Huntington pointed out that while the term "professional" has taken on differing meanings and connotations in western society, his definition of a professional is akin to that of a doctor or lawyer, based upon "prolonged education and experience," with the

---

[20] Ibid.
[21] Ibid., 85.
[22] Ibid., 7-10.

foundation and drive for such a vocation based not on monetary gain, but on "a higher calling in the service of society."[23]

Huntington described the professional expertise exhibited by the military as the "management of violence." This expertise distinguishes the military profession from that of other overlapping trades and vocations found in the civilian world (e.g. engineers, mechanics, and pilots). While one can master other civilian vocations and skill sets by learning techniques and procedures, Huntington argued that the essence of military professionalism required the broad mastery of many techniques and procedures, but more importantly, it involved the understanding of history, the dynamic culture and society it defends, and other less tangible skills and variables that influence and play a role in the successful management of violence.[24]

U.S. society is obviously keenly interested in the protection and security provided to it by a professional military. As Huntington put it, just like a patient or client depends upon and trusts the skill and professionalism of a doctor or lawyer, so too does society at large trust and depend on the military for its security. However, while a doctor or lawyer affects only those patients or clients within their hire, the military alone is responsible for the collective security of society as a whole. This unique characteristic combines what Huntington labeled a unique blend of skill and responsibility that set the military profession apart from other professions.[25] Huntington argued that it was this uniqueness that also motivated the military officer. While other professions draw much larger monetary compensation resulting in motivation to excel and further themselves in their profession, the military professional's motivation stems more from their obligation,

---

[23] Ibid., 8.
[24] Ibid., 14.
[25] Ibid., 15.

responsibility, and "sense of duty" to serve society. As Huntington put it, "The motivations of the officer are a technical love for his craft and the sense of social obligation to utilize this craft for the benefit of society."[26]

Similar to the doctor and patient, responsibilities and rules bound the relationship between the military and the state. Huntington likened this relationship to that of an "expert advisor," where the military's interests and expertise involve only those activities specific to the cause at hand, "...explaining only to his client his needs in this area, advising him as to how to meet these needs, and then when the client has made his decisions, aid him in implementing them."[27] Huntington stated this "explicit code" is comparable to the "ethic" espoused by other professions, but within the military, this code is more expressed in terms of "custom, tradition, and the continuing spirit of the profession."[28]

Huntington argued that as the professionalism within the military increased, the functional imperative would be better served and the organization itself would take on characteristics consistent with "conservative realism" that would then better provide security to the liberal society it served and protected.[29] Huntington believed those that shared this "conservative" worldview possessed what he referred to as the "military mind," elements of which included:

> ...a belief in the fallibility of man and the permanence of conflict in human affairs, an appreciation for history, a belief in the historical cycles rather than progress, an emphasis on the primacy of the group over the individual, a focus on the state as the fundamental unit of political organization and on the centrality of power in the international relations, an emphasis on the immediacy of the threat and worst case analyses, bias

---

[26] Ibid., 15.
[27] Ibid., 16.
[28] Ibid.
[29] Nielsen and Snider, *American Civil-Military Relations*, 6.

toward strong forces-in-being and skepticism of alliances, a desire to avoid initialing conflict unless victory is assured, and hostility toward military adventurism.[30]

Huntington's theory of objective control remained unchallenged for nearly fifteen years. As America's war in Vietnam entered its second decade and immense internal divisiveness over the conflict roiled the nation, a countervailing theory appeared.

Morris Janowitz – Convergence Theory

Morris Janowitz was a noted sociologist and political scientist who published *The Professional Soldier* in 1971. Like Huntington, Janowitz proposed a civil-military relations theory that sought to explain the dynamics of the relationship within the context of the Cold War and propose a course of action that he felt would best harmonize the civil-military relationship and enhance to nation's future security. Janowitz's argument would stand in stark contrast to that of Huntington. While Huntington argued for ensuring completely separate spheres between military expertise and civilian control, Janowitz argued for the complete opposite. Janowitz saw the post-World War II era and the Cold War as driven largely by a new spectrum of warfare that called for increased "convergence" between society, civilian leaders, and the military. He felt this requirement for convergence between the military and civilian spheres called for a new type of security force, one Janowitz referred to as the "constabulary force."

Like Huntington, Janowitz viewed the potential of "high-tech total war" and America's policy of deterrence as activities the military must stand ready to execute for the long term. However, while the nuclear age drove the military to be technically proficient and ready to carry out the nuclear strikes underpinning the concept of

---

[30] Ibid.

deterrence, he foresaw the U.S. engaged in a series of emerging limited wars that would drive the military toward the constabulary concept. Janowitz argued that, "…the military establishment becomes a constabulary force when it is continuously prepared to act, committed to the minimum use of force, and seeks viable international relations, rather than victory because it has incorporated a protective military posture."[31] In other words, he argued the potential destructive power and the totality of nuclear weapons would inherently shift U.S. security policy toward a new "posture" of peacekeeping that would, in effect, act to limit conflict and potential escalation. Janowitz argued that the age of strategic nuclear deterrence would now put the U.S. in a position that would "operate on a double standard of peacetime and wartime standards," and believed that in order to operate effectively, changes would have to be made in the way the military and civilian leaders interacted. In order to deal effectively with this dilemma, Janowitz suggested the movement away from the traditional military concept, and a move more towards that of a constabulary force.

Janowitz viewed the extreme end of the threat continuum that dealt with nuclear war and strategic deterrence as driven more by overall national strategy and posturing than military expertise. While the military needed to be "technically proficient" to employ nuclear weapons if necessary, he believed this level of war required a limited amount of technical "expertise." Therefore, within the nuclear realm, Janowitz argued that civil-military interplay centered more on the numbers of weapons, their placement, and their political application, with the employment of nuclear tactics being very straightforward and clear-cut.[32] Janowitz believed this expertise contrasted with the

---

[31] Morris Janowitz, *The Professional Soldier* (New York: Collier Macmillian Publishers, 1971), 418.
[32] Ibid.

requirements to be successful at the other end of the threat spectrum, which dealt with the

complexity of "flexible" and "specialized" engagements future non-nuclear limited wars

would require.

Janowitz, who wrote towards the latter half of the Vietnam conflict, argued that in

order to deal with the more likely broad range of potential limited engagements, a

constabulary force would "provide a continuity with past military experiences and

traditions, but also offer a basis for the radical adaptation of the profession" and would

therefore, be proficient in serving a broad range of military power and organizations,

ranging from nuclear war to military aid programs to counter-guerilla warfare.[33] This

constabulary force would then "eliminate the distinction between the peacetime and

wartime military establishment," and would move the military more toward the role of an

international police force than that of the "warrior."[34] Like a standard military force,

Janowitz argued the constabulary force would be ready to operate on the

"straightforward" high end of nuclear operations and deterrence, but would be better

prepared to deal with limited wars and peacekeeping missions--the area where he saw the

greatest potential for conflict and where the U.S. had failed recently (e.g., Vietnam).

Janowitz believed these future conflicts (short of nuclear war) would require "enlarged

politico-military responsibility"[35] and would drive the need for a greater homogenization

of societal sentiment, civilian direction and policy, international politics, and military

expertise--requirements he felt the constabulary force would be better prepared to deliver.

Janowitz believed that merging the civilian and military spheres would better

align and synchronize societal values with the military and in doing so, better serve the

---

[33] Ibid., 418.
[34] Feaver, "The Civil-Military Problematique," 164.
[35] Janowitz, *The Professional Soldier*, liv.

15

military by facilitating "clearer" policy interpretations for implementation--something Huntington labeled as "subjective control." The move toward the constabulary force, Janowitz believed, would cultivate a collaborative sense among the military and civilian leadership, yielding a type of civilian control that was more "self-imposed" rather than via "rule of law" that Huntington's model presupposed. Out of this "higher level" of civilian control, Janowitz believed the military would better understand and deal with the ambiguities associated with the limited wars and hazy conflict resolution of the future. He believed that such a constabulary force could be developed by moving away from the selective service and moving towards an all-volunteer military force, something he felt would increase the type of "military professionalism" essential to the constabulary construct.[36] Janowitz felt this constabulary force would be more aligned and synchronized politically with civilian leadership and with overall societal attitudes and ideals. Janowitz would go on to say, "The officer in the constabulary force is particularly attuned to withstand the pressures of constant alerts and tension. He is sensitive to the political and social impact of the military establishment on international security affairs."[37]

Janowitz argued the opposite of what Huntington suggested was the best model to ensure sound civilian control and military effectiveness. While Huntington's model of objective control aimed to limit societal influence and civilian meddling in order to increase effectiveness, Janowitz argued that a new age of potential limited and protracted wars called for a greater convergence of societal values, civilian leadership, and military

---

[36] Ibid., 418-422.
[37] Ibid., 419.

norms. This convergence, Janowitz opined, would better serve the nation in the "grey area" of conflict he saw on the horizon (illustrated in Figure 2).

Janowitz agreed that blurring the line separating the military and civilian spheres would raise new issues and challenges regarding civilian control. He admitted that asking military leaders to be more involved in national politics and policy application might increase an officer's "frustration." To mitigate any potential military frustration with civilian control, Janowitz offered suggestions to civilian leadership authorities: 1) Limit military goals to feasible and attainable objectives; 2) Assist in the formulation of military doctrine so that it becomes a more unified expression of national policies objectives; 3) Maintain a sense of professional self-esteem in the military, and 4) Develop

---

[38] Figure is my individual interpretation of Convergence Theory, derived from Janowitz, *The Professional Soldier*, vii-lvi.

new devices for the exercise of political control.[39] While these control measures would obviously aid in ensuring that a constabulary force served the intent of the civilian leadership, Janowitz also called for measures and criteria by which military performance was measured through increased civilian oversight into the budget process, the allocation of roles and missions, and military involvement in the advice and recommendations to the President of foreign policy issues.[40]

Both Huntington and Janowitz refer to "professionalism" as the key ingredient and primary control mechanism in their respective models for effective military security and civilian control.[41] However, while Huntington's idea of military professionalism centers around the professional ethic derived from the primacy of the military's autonomy and respected expertise in the "management of violence," Janowitz's version stems from the question he proposes--"why do officer's fight?"[42] While both definitions of professionalism share broad similarities, Janowitz sees military professionalism (and the answer to the question above) originating more from the savvy embodiment of a "professional constabulary officer," that is, socially and politically aware, confident, and an expert in successfully operating in an environment with overlapping institutional systems that blend societal values, politics, policy and military expertise.[43] Put another way, Janowitz envisioned a military officer corps that mirrored society, that is paid competitively with respect to other societal professionals, but embodied with a distinct military "service ethic."

---

[39] Ibid., 435.
[40] Feaver, "The Civil-Military Problematique," 164-165.
[41] Ibid.
[42] Janowitz, *The Professional Soldier*, 440.
[43] Feaver, "The Civil-Military Problematique," 165-166.

Peter Feaver – Agency Theory

While the theories of Huntington and Janowitz touch on the civil-military issue from a broad and perhaps generic perspective, neither delves into the functional day-to-day relationship and the mechanics of how the civil-military relationship actually works. In 2003, Peter Feaver would offer an additional civil-military model, and would attempt to answer the more functional question: "How *do* civilians control the military?"[44]

Theories of objective or subjective control aside, given the U.S. military's venerable size, strength and overwhelming coercive power, how *does* the U.S. civilian authority control the military, ensuring the military follow its orders and carries out its wishes? In *Armed Servants: Agency, Oversight, and Civil-Military Relations*, Feaver describes the "Principal-Agent Framework" as a vehicle for civilian control and offers a theory--referred to as "Agency Theory" that he believes better explains changes in civil-military relations in both the Cold War and post-Cold War era.[45] Feaver's theory centers on the same issues discussed by both Huntington and Janowitz, specifically "how to control a military strong enough to do anything the civilians ask with a military subordinate enough to do only what civilians authorize."[46] This dilemma plays out again in familiar ground--how much military autonomy and trust is allowed without undermining civilian authority, and conversely, how much oversight can civilian leaders impose without degrading and negatively impacting military effectiveness and morale? This relationship and the pragmatic mechanics of the everyday interaction between

---

[44] Peter D. Feaver, *Armed Servants: Agency, Oversight, and Civil-Military Relations* (Cambridge: Harvard University Press, 2005), 1. (emphasis added)

[45] Ibid.

[46] Ibid., 2.

civilian and military leaders is what Feaver examines "deductively" and explains through recent studies in other (non-security) bureaucracies.[47]

Feaver argues that, "…the essence of civil-military relations is a strategic interaction between civilian principals and military agents. Civilians decide how to monitor the military, based on varying expectations they hold about whether or not the military will obey them faithfully in the particulars of what they ask."[48] Feaver borrows from other scholarly literature published on the Principal-Agent Framework, which describes this interaction as "working" and "shirking." He looks at the civil-military puzzle in terms of describing the conditions that would lead to intrusive versus non-intrusive oversight by the civilian principle, and when, and under what conditions could one expect the military agent to either, "work" or "shirk." Feaver submits that in understanding this framework, predictions can be made as to the level of conduct and effectiveness of the day-to-day civil-military relationship.[49]

Feaver argues the principal-agent framework, developed by economists, is well-suited to address the mannerisms of the civil-military relationship due to two distinctive characteristics: hierarchy and strategic interaction.[50] The hierarchy stems from the democratically-derived civilian authority over the military. The interaction between the two entities is "strategic" because, as Feaver puts it, "…the choices civilians make are contingent on their expectations of what the military is likely to do, and the visa versa."[51]

Feaver begins explaining his use of agency theory by first looking back at the predictions made by Huntington and the impact the Cold War would have on the [then]

---

[47] Ibid.
[48] Ibid.
[49] Ibid.
[50] Ibid., 54.
[51] Ibid.

present day civil-military relationship. Huntington argued that in the long term, unless the U.S. adopted his prescription of a conservative shift in values and objective control over the military, American society's liberal values and influence would negatively impact the effectiveness of the military and the ability to prevail in the Cold War era. Feaver argues that despite not adopting Huntington's prescriptions, the U.S. did prevail in the Cold War era, and therefore he argues, that there must be a more precise and "empirical" alternative explanation for civil-military relational outcomes over time. Feaver's concept moves away from broad theoretical strokes of measuring the civil-military relationship in terms of "winning or losing" or "coup or no coup" to the "more general phenomenon of political principals seeking to monitor and influence the behavior of their political agents."[52]

Feaver's theory blends two generic concepts. The first is that agents (in this case the military) will "work" when monitored and will "shirk" when not monitored. Therefore, the principal (civilian leadership) must develop the most effective and efficient way to monitor the agent to ensure the agent is carrying out the wishes of the principal. These monitoring mechanisms can be intrusive or non-intrusive. The second concept deals with the inherent inefficiency of constantly monitoring your agent and that the best solution to ensure "optimal compliance" is to improve the quality of the agent, finding solutions that bring the agent's preferences more in line with that of the principal.[53] Feaver's theory explores and blends both of these premises, investigating periods of intrusive and non-intrusive civilian monitoring of the military and how that affected the alignment of preferences and efficiency between the principal and agent.

---

[52] Ibid., 284.
[53] Ibid., 56.

21

Feaver's model of "working" or "shirking" in the principal/agent context of the civil-military relationship is quite simple. Society elects and empowers civilians (the principal) with the responsibly to provide security for the population. The civilian leadership in turn contracts the military (its agent) to carry out that mission on its behalf. The principal then decides on the required control measures and monitoring mechanisms to ensure the agent is properly carrying out the delegated responsibilities, taking into account the cost and effort of such monitoring. Feaver points out that complete delegation may result in an agent free to do whatever it wishes (potentially resulting in shirking). Conversely, the principal-agent interaction could be so restrictive and monitor-intensive that it undermines the agreed upon relationship and delegation of duties.[54] Feaver argues that the optimal monitoring system is one that "minimizes the incentives and opportunities to flout the principal's wishes, at the least cost to the principal, while preserving the efficiencies of the specialization that come with delegation."[55]

The terms "working" and "shirking" may hold with them a negative connotation in the context of describing the honorable military profession and its interaction with civilian leadership. Feaver acknowledges this, and states that it is of course "reasonable to posit that both the civilian principals and the military agents want the same thing: security for the state. They can, however, disagree on how to provide that security, in general and especially in particular settings."[56] In other words, the generic terms of "working" and "shirking" take on more dynamic and multidimensional characteristics when applying them within the civil-military context. Feaver takes this further and describes "working" as doing things the civilians want, and "shirking" as doing things the

---

[54] Ibid., 57.
[55] Ibid.
[56] Ibid.

22

way that the military wants and desires.[57] Refined even further, Feaver states that "working" within this context "involves a good faith effort to represent the principal's interests. Put another way, "working" is the ideal conduct that the agent would perform *if* the principal had full knowledge of what the agent could do and was in fact doing."[58] "Shirking" then, would be anything less than an ideal "good faith effort" on the part of the agent to represent the principal's interests. In this case, the agent's personal or organizational preferences or opinions diverge in varying degrees, causing the agent's efforts to potentially stray from the principal's vision.

Feaver breaks down the civil-military relationship into two key goals. The "functional" goal of the military agent to provide an "action," in this case appropriate (as seen by the principal) security for the nation on behalf of the principal civilian leaders, and the "relational" goal, which describes the "ideal" interplay between the principal and the agent leading to appropriate security measures consistent with the intent of the principal.[59] Within the context of these definitions, if both goals are met positively, then the military agent is indeed "working"; conversely, anything short of, or negativity impacting these two goals, will be perceived as a degree of "shirking," scaled to the level of discourse and divergence between the principal and agent.[60] This continuum of "working" and "shirking" is bounded by two extremes: on one end a military coup, and on the other, an agent that successfully carries out the intent of the principal "vigorously and without subversion."[61]

---

[57] Ibid.
[58] Ibid.
[59] Ibid., 61.
[60] Ibid., 62.
[61] Ibid.

When applying the "working" or "shirking" framework in the actual day-to-day mechanics of civil-military relations, it is obviously much less black and white than as laid out above. Certainly, the civilian principal and the military agent must rely on a dialog and an exchange of information to execute operations and provide security for the nation. Just as the military relies on the civilian leadership to provide direction, civilians rely on the expertise of the military to advise and provide recommendations. If the civilian principal proposes a course of action to which the military agent knows that they cannot deliver or feels will have a counter effect to that which the principal envisions, and that discussion leads to a change of direction or differing proposed course by the principal, then one should *not* view this as shirking. As Feaver puts it:

> Shirking is not synonymous with persuading a civilian policymaker to change his mind. Thus, evaluating whether shirking has occurred or not occurred is not as simple as discovering whether military advice was followed. Rather, it involves judgments about the integrity of the military advice itself as well as judgments about the conditions under which civilians changed their minds.[62]

"Shirking," in the context of the above example, would lead from allowing the military agent's *own* divergent preferences to influence and interfere with the exchange in a manner in which undermines and subverts the spirit and faithfulness of the functional and rational goals. These agent-divergent (and perhaps selfish) preferences may center around what policy or decision best serves the military interests or how much undesired principal monitoring the agent anticipates with respect to a particular proposed course of action.[63]

Once the principal issues clear direction to the agent, the civilian principles must then decide the degree to which they will monitor their military agents (non-intrusively or

---

[62] Ibid., 284.
[63] Ibid., 63.

24

intrusively) to ensure they are faithfully carrying out the principal's intent. The principle bases the degree and method of monitoring on many factors, including the importance or complexity of the operation, the amount of trust or perceived divergence in views between the principal and agent, and the potential that an excessive cost of monitoring may outweigh the benefits.

Feaver argues that with the control measures in place, the military agent then operates on the "work or shirk continuum," based on expectations, the degree to which preferences align between the principal and agent, and perhaps the agent's potential consequences for "shirking." The more divergent the principal and agent's preferences are, the more likely the agent is to "shirk," and accordingly, the more the principal is apt to induce intrusive monitoring to ensure the principle's intent is carried out (illustrated in Figure 3 below).

---

[64] Figure is my individual interpretation of Agency Theory, derived from Feaver, *Armed Servants*, 58-68.

An example of this would be a military officer's (agent) perceived difference of opinion with civilian direction (principal) to proceed down a particular course of action. Because of the perceived divergence in preferences, the principle institutes intrusive monitoring to ensure the agent is indeed "working" in line with what the principle expects. This example may indeed end in a "functional success," but may come at a "relational cost" between the principal and agent, damaging trust and perhaps hampering future efficiency. Conversely, we can see how this scenario potentially plays out with the same diverging preferences, but without intrusive monitoring. Here, despite the divergence, the agent carries out the task free from intrusive monitoring. This results in less friction and "relational success" between the principal and agent, but due to the preference divergence, lack of monitoring, and autonomy provided to the agent, the employed means or end state may not be representative of the principal's intentions.

Feaver then offers four potential outcomes derived from the degree of principal monitoring and military working or shirking: 1) military working under non-intrusive monitoring, 2) military working under intrusive monitoring, 3) military shirking under non-intrusive monitoring, and 4) military shirking under intrusive monitoring.[65] Obviously, under optimal conditions, having the preferences of the principal and the agent perfectly aligned would result in the most effective system with the military working and the agent monitoring by non-intrusive means (if at all). Certainly, we can agree that this is seldom the case. While the U.S. military and civilian leadership may enjoy periods of complete synchronization, the relationship and inter-workings of the mechanics of the day-to-day relationship usually fall within the spectrum described above. This, as Feaver puts it, is the civil-military "strategic interaction" that plays out

---

[65] Ibid., 284.

26

on a daily basis.[66] Thus, Feaver's agency theory offers something unique and different from what Huntington and Janowitz offered, and "…treats civil-military relations as a special case of the more general phenomenon of political principals seeking to monitor and influence the behavior of their political agents."[67]

Feaver's agency theory centers around one side of the civil-military relationship-- mechanisms to ensure civilian control of the military.[68] Feaver points out that within our democratic system, voters elect and entrust civilian leaders to create policy and do what they think is best to ensure national security. Those civilian leaders in turn, rely on military officers (when necessary) to carry out prescribed tasks and responsibilities consistent with their priorities and policies. While military preferences and opinions may not align completely (or at all) with that of civilian leadership, Feaver points out that, "civilian principles are to be obeyed even when they are wrong about what is needed for national security," emphasizing that, "civilians have the right be wrong." However, Feaver goes on to say that while obeying the whims of a "foolish" principal may indeed be classified as "working," it is not necessarily synonymous with meeting the needs of national security.[69] The misapplication of military power by an uninformed or mislead principal can indeed undermine national security. Certainly, in order to wield military force effectively, both the principal and agent must enter into a collaborative relationship to ensure expertise and expectations are shared on both ends. Feaver refers to this dilemma as the "civil-military challenge," where, on the extreme end, "military experts educate civilian amateurs before civilian ignorance damages national security--and to do

---

[66] Ibid.
[67] Ibid.
[68] Ibid., 298.
[69] Ibid.

so without undermining the role of the civilian as the principal"[70] In this case, fostering a high degree of trust and spirit of collaboration which draws from both civilian and military expertise is essential--and by no means an easy task.

Indeed, this "civil-military challenge" has implications at a higher level that are underscored by Feaver's question: "Are civilians more likely to be wrong on the important matters of national security?"[71] Feaver sites many sources that subscribe to the "normative" implication of the civil-military relationship--that delegation of responsibility to the military, followed with nonintrusive monitoring, provides the best assurance that the military can translate civilian's orders into successful national security.[72] Feaver sides with others and believes that while the above example may hold true in certain circumstances, "the proper limits of delegation are best determined not by military expertise but by political calculation."[73] In other words, principals must understand where military expertise begins and ends--where civilians are (and should be) "better positioned to judge the political underpinnings of military policy," and where military officers are better at judging and guiding the potential military means agreed upon to achieve that policy.[74]

Shaping a Civil-Military Framework

Certainly, these three theories do not serve to summarize or attempt to define completely the complexity of the civil-military relationship. Rather, they are offered as a starting point for the reader to begin to shape a framework in his or her mind from which

---

[70] Ibid.
[71] Ibid., 300.
[72] Ibid.
[73] Ibid.
[74] Ibid.

to base the civil-military discussion upon. Each has offered a different and unique view at what factors, trends, and mechanisms affect the civil-military relational balance and the subsequent security it provides to the nation. Understanding and having an appreciation for each theory offered will help in the next section as we explore case studies of eras and engagements where the civil-military relationship was less than optimal.

Of the authors outlined thus far, Samuel Huntington offered the first notable framework and theory in the study of civil-military relations. He saw the post-World War II Soviet threat as a long term issue that would threaten American security if the U.S. failed to transform and build a more permanent and professional military force with "a properly balanced pattern" of civil-military relations. He argued this balance is always affected by two constants--the functional imperative of society's requirement to field a military force to provide security for the nation, and the influence of the societal imperative, where dynamic societal values, culture and sentiment, resident within those military members, society, and civilian leaders, inherently impact and shape the civil-military relationship. Huntington argued the most effective way to achieve a balance between these two imperatives, and therefore best harmonize the civil-military relationship and maximize security, was through objective control of the military.

Under objective control, the military serves strictly as an instrument of the state, is apolitical in nature, and has the autonomy that Huntington argued best increased professionalism and best served the functional imperative of protecting the state. Contrary to the idea of objective control, subjective control seeks to politicize the military, making the military one with society, and is driven largely by civilian power groups seeking to leverage the military into conformance with their competing views and

29

interests.[75] Huntington viewed subjective control as having a negative impact on long-term military effectiveness and security.[76]

Huntington viewed the idea of "military professionalism" as the key to objective control. Under this construct, military officers were respected experts and advisors in the "management of violence," sharing the same values of "expertise, responsibility and corporateness" as other respected professions (e.g., doctors and lawyers) characterized and manifested by prolonged education and experience. Huntington's civil-military model of functional and societal imperatives, functional and societal control, and professionalism shaped the civil-military debate and catalyzed the actions of other theorists of civil-military relations. The impact of Huntington and objective control is a misplaced belief in some military circles that the autonomy enjoyed by the military extends to the conduct of battle. In other words, once civilian leaders determine the political end state, they should cede all further discussions and action to the military. The often heard military refrain of "give me the mission, don't tell me how to do it" exemplifies this common misunderstanding of objective control.

Both Janowitz and Huntington agreed that the Cold War era would bring about new military challenges and influence the way that civilian leadership interacted with and controlled its military force. Janowitz believed the totality of nuclear war would blur the lines separating peacetime and wartime and would call for a new type of military force that would be proficient at operating across a vast spectrum of engagements.[77] While the new era would require the military to remain proficient in the high-end nuclear realm, he

---

[75] Huntington, *The Soldier and the State*, 5.
[76] Ibid.
[77] Janowitz, *The Professional Soldier*, 419.

30

viewed involvement in limited and protracted "policing" engagements as requiring a differing mindset and "type" of military officer and expertise.

Janowitz argued that in order for the military to operate successfully in its new international policing role, it needed to be more in tune with societal values and "civilianized" in order to be effective. While both Janowitz and Huntington agreed that the standing military force was inherently conservative, Janowitz disagreed with Huntington and believed that a more liberal force that was sensitive to and more representative of the liberal society it protected would be more synchronized and in-step with its civilian leadership, and therefore more effective at operating within the new policing role. This new constabulary force, which Janowitz argued would be most effective, would then operate more or less under the model that Huntington felt would be least effective, which was "subjective control."

Janowitz agreed with Huntington that military professionalism was critical and beneficial to the civil-military relationship. While Huntington's idea of professionalism is gleaned from autonomy, unique expertise and limited outside civilian intervention, Janowitz's version stems more from the exigencies of the Cold War environment, the requirement for the military to become more civilianized, and what he saw as the new role of the constabulary officer.

> The constabulary officer performs his duties, which includes fighting, because he is a professional with a sense of self-esteem and moral worth. Civilian society permits him to maintain his code of honor and encourages him to develop his professional skill. He is amenable to civilian political control because he recognizes that civilians appreciate and understand the tasks and responsibilities of the constabulary forces. He is integrated into civilian society because he shares its common values.[78]

---

[78] Ibid., 440.

Janowitz's model and view of how to best manage civil-military relations in the Cold War era would stand in stark contrast to that proposed by Samuel Huntington. Both models serve as opposing "bookends" to the vast spectrum of thought surrounding the discussion of civil-military relations. With Janowitz and Huntington "framing" the civil-military relational debate, other theories have emerged that draw from both and continue to examine the nuances of this crucial relationship.

While the theories of Huntington and Janowitz centered on "macro" institutional and societal influences, Feaver's agency theory examined the civil-military relationship from an "empirical" lens, offering an explanation of how the relationship actually works on a daily basis. Feaver argues that although the overall perception of civil-military affairs within the U.S. is positive and the idea of civilian control of the military remains well established, its "principle means" may be contested.[79] Feaver believes that the U.S. is experiencing a new "norm" among American military officers that moves away from the idea that inherent in civilian control is the civilian leader's "right to be wrong."[80] He goes on to say that within the realm of decision-making concerning the use of military force, military officers "see no inconsistency between endorsing civilian control and endorsing an 'insist' role for the military, where 'insist' implies accept our advice or else we will shirk or resign in protest."[81] Feaver points out that this attitude is not "contempt" for the principle of civilian control itself, rather a concern that to do otherwise ("work" in this case), would pose a risk to national security.[82] This type of "shirking," even if helping to ensure security, still undermines the idea of civilian control, and as Feaver puts

---

[79] Feaver, *Armed Servants*, 300.
[80] Ibid.
[81] Ibid.
[82] Ibid.

it, "threatens to hold the civilian principle hostage to the preferences of the military agent."[83] Feaver takes this a step further and likens this example to "mutiny" on the battlefield, where one "resigns in protest," and has the same "poisonous effect" on the civil-military relationship as a "mutiny" would on the battlefield.[84]

It is certainly in America's best interests to limit civil-military relational friction and harness our collective power to ensure security of the nation. Feaver points out that although the military has an obligation to "work," the civilian counterparts have an even greater obligation to "fulfill their role responsibly."[85] He states that although the ultimate responsibility for the management of the military lies in the hands of the civilian leaders, society's voters retain the final say in who those leaders are, and should closely monitor how that relationship and its effects on security play out.[86] Feaver sums it up this way:

> History shows that the military is not as "right" in civil-military disputes as the military triumphalists might suppose. But even when the military is right, democratic theory intervenes and insists that it submit to the civilian leadership that the polity has chosen. Let civilian voters punish civilian leaders for wrong decisions. Let the military advise against foolish adventures, even advising strenuously when circumstances demand. But let the military execute those orders faithfully. The republic would be better served even by foolish working than by enlightened shirking.[87]

Each author has offered a different and unique view of what factors, trends, and mechanisms affect the civil-military relational balance and the subsequent security it provides to the nation. Understanding and having an appreciation for each theory offered will help in the next section that explores case studies of eras and engagements where the civil-military relationship was less than optimal.

---

[83] Ibid., 301.
[84] Ibid.
[85] Ibid., 302.
[86] Ibid.
[87] Ibid.

CHAPTER 2: CASE STUDIES

Korea

The end of World War II and the dawn of the nuclear era placed America in unfamiliar territory as a major world power. While the U.S. struggled to formulate an emerging nuclear strategy and deal with the beginnings of the Cold War, it also had to balance the inevitable drawdown from the vast surplus of equipment and personnel amassed to fight World War II. While the increase of lethality on the atomic battlefield advanced, all other elements of military readiness declined precipitously. The defense budget dropped from approximately $90 billion in 1945 to a very low $13 billion in 1950.[1] Most significantly, the conventional U.S. military went from trained and ready in 1945 to untrained and unprepared for anything other than guarding airbases for nuclear-armed bombers.[2] In short, the U.S. was not at all prepared to enter a another conventional fight only a few years after using the atomic bomb to help bring an end to World War II.

In August 1945, the defeat of the Japanese had left Korea divided at the 38th parallel, the result a "temporary" agreement reached between the U.S. and the U.S.S.R. to act as dual-occupying trustees in the interim, while the country held elections to reunify the peninsula. With the U.S. supporting Syngman Rhee in the South and the U.S.S.R. backing Kim Il Song in the North, tensions rose and trust between the U.S. and U.S.S.R.

---

[1] Vardell Nesmith, "The Korean War" (Lecture, Joint Advanced Warfighting School, Norfolk, VA, 1 October 2010).

[2] Robert Previdi, *Civilian Control Versus Military Rule* (New York, New York: Hippocrene Books, Inc., 1988), 51.

eroded. On 25 June 1950, in a bold move that caught the U.S. by surprise, the North

Korean Army marched across the 38th parallel and invaded South Korea.

A former World War I Artillery Captain and "no-nonsense" businessman,

President Harry S. Truman had always believed in strong civilian control and felt that the

President must be the absolute commander of the country's armed forces. "He believed

he should set guidelines for the military, approve their strategy and major tactical

recommendations when proper, and see to it that they implemented the policies of the

administration."[3] In the new atomic age, the immense devastation possible from a single

weapon reinforced and underscored the significance of civilian control. As the first

President to authorize the use of a nuclear weapon, he understood first-hand the level of

attention to military matters the current era demanded. In Truman's words, "I took the

position that the president, as the commander-in-chief, had to know everything that was

going on. I had just enough experience to know that if you are not careful, the military

will hedge you in."[4]

Earlier in 1948, the Joint Chiefs cautioned Truman that, "the United States should

not become so irrevocably involved in the Korean situation that an action taken by any

faction in Korea or by any other power in Korea (e.g., Soviet Union) could be considered

a 'casus belli' (justification for war) for the United States."[5] Certainly, in the developing

Cold War with the Soviets, any mismanaged military escalation on the Korean peninsula

could spark a larger war, one that the U.S. wanted to avoid. The North Korean invasion

put the U.S. and President Truman in a tough position. On the one hand, allowing the

---

[3] Richard Haynes, *The Awesome Power* (Baton Rouge: Louisiana State University Press, 1973), 30-31.

[4] Harry S Truman, *Memoirs: Years of Trial and Hope* (Garden City: Doubleday, 1955), 88.

[5] Dale R. Herspring, *The Pentagon and the Presidency* (Lawrence: The University Press of Kansas, 2005), 73.

North Koreans to advance and take the South would lead to greater communist influence in the region and potentially act as the catalyst for the next world war. One the other hand, any U.S. backed military opposition to the North's advance must be done prudently and in a fashion as to not escalate into a full-scale conflict that would involve the Soviets.[6]

At the time of the invasion, General Douglas MacArthur, now a five star general, was stationed in Japan and serving as both the Theater Commander and the Supreme Commander of all Allied Powers, charged with rebuilding Japan and overseeing the installation of a democratic system of government. General MacArthur, having fought in both World War I and II and received the Medal of Honor for his defense of the Philippines, was admired by a majority of Americans and seen as a war hero. At the time of the Korean attack, John Dulles, the U.S. delegate to the United Nations and later the U.S. Secretary of State, was in Japan with Gen MacArthur, reporting back to Washington that the general was "so despondent" of the situation that he should be immediately withdrawn from his post.[7] President Truman disagreed, believing that the general "was so politically involved in the country…he could not recall MacArthur without causing a tremendous reaction."[8] Following a U.N. Resolution authorizing the U.S. to halt the North's aggression south of the 38th parallel, MacArthur took command of Allied Forces in the escalating conflict.

Due to the low state of U.S. military readiness, the Joint Chiefs and the Secretary of Defense were not in favor of committing ground troops in Korea.[9] On 25 June 1950,

---

[6] Ibid., 74.
[7] Ibid.
[8] Ibid.
[9] Previdi, *Civilian Control Versus Military Rule*, 53.

Truman had authorized both air and naval strikes on advancing North Korean tanks, with less than favorable results. After visiting the front lines, General MacArthur (on his own authority) authorized air strikes north of the 38th parallel and sent President Truman a message stating the only way to hold the present line would be by sending in U.S. ground troops.[10] Reluctantly, the Joint Chiefs agreed and advised President Truman to deploy a small number of "reinforcing" troops. Still Chairman of the Joint Chiefs, Omar Bradley, worried about America's involvement and the potential for a "no-win" situation, stating now famously, "Korea is the wrong war, at the wrong time, in the wrong place."[11] Secretary of Defense Louis Johnson also opposed placing ground troops in Korea and advocated "keeping a tight rein on MacArthur," warning Truman that MacArthur's instructions "should be so detailed so as not to give him too much discretion."[12]

Even with the introduction of U.S. ground forces, the situation in Korea began to deteriorate. With limited resources and a quickly advancing enemy, General MacArthur contacted Washington with a plan to conduct an amphibious landing at Inchon, near Seoul, and outflank the stalled North Koreans. If successful, it would catch the North Koreans completely by surprise, disrupt rear supply lines, and force the enemy to fight on two fronts.[13] While the plan was initially touted as just another MacArthur "harebrained scheme," MacArthur was charismatic and thorough enough to convince the Joint Chiefs, who still retained doubts over its plausibility, to support the plan.[14]

On 17 September 1950, Allied troops landed at Inchon and achieved an overwhelming victory, putting the North Koreans on the run and recapturing the South

---

[10] Herspring, *The Pentagon and the Presidency,* 74.
[11] Ibid., 75.
[12] Joseph Goulden, *Korea: The Untold Story of the War* (New York: Times Books, 1982), 67.
[13] Ibid.
[14] Ibid.,76.

Korean capital.[15] Although some North Korean fighters had escaped to the north, the North Korean Army had been effectively decisively defeated and would no longer pose a military threat to the south.[16]

Without clear political or strategic direction from the onset of the conflict, the question then became what to do next. Prior to the Inchon invasion, General MacArthur had told General Collins (Army Chief of Staff) that it was his intention to defeat all of North Korea.[17] After the counterattack at Inchon and subsequent exploitation, Truman directed General MacArthur to "conduct the necessary military operations either to force the North Koreans behind the 38th parallel, or destroy their forces" and to "cease ground operations if either the Soviet or Communist Chinese enter the fray."[18] This order would become a major point of contention between MacArthur and Truman. MacArthur firmly believed in the complete defeat of the North and the reunification of Korea under a non-communist regime, and welcomed any provocation with the newly Communist China it may generate. MacArthur not only wanted to defeat the North Koreans, he wanted to change the strategic balance in the region by defeating Communist China on the battlefield.[19] Truman began to feel the pressure at home, as Republican Senator William Knowland began politicizing the war and demanding complete military and political defeat of North Korea.[20]

Truman, feeling more and more detached from ongoing operations and receiving political heat as mid-term elections approached, decided to arrange a meeting on 15

---

[15] Ibid.
[16] Ibid.
[17] Ibid.
[18] David Rees, *Korea: The Limited War* (New York: St. Martin's Press, 1964), 100.
[19] Previdi, *Civilian Control Versus Military Rule*, 63.
[20] Herspring, *The Pentagon and the Presidency*, 77.

October1950 with MacArthur on Wake Island to ensure that they understood each other's intentions. At the meeting, President Truman expressed his concerns that in no way did he want U.S. actions in the north to spur a Chinese reaction and force them to intervene.[21] General MacArthur assured the President that his operations would not coerce the Chinese into becoming involved. On 17 October 1950, just two days after his meeting with President Truman, and without stating his intentions or gaining approval, MacArthur launched an offensive and moved past the northern boundary established by the Joint Chiefs for U.S. operations. Under MacArthur's direction, U.S. forces would capture the North Korean capital city of Pyongyang (100 miles south of the Yalu River and border of China) on 19 October 1950.[22] While the Chiefs were displeased because MacArthur had strict orders to only allow South Korean soldiers to approach the Chinese border, "...the Chiefs did nothing. They were dealing with a national hero, a winner, and everyone was afraid of moving against him."[23] MacArthur's actions would indeed drive the Chinese into action and have dire consequences for the U.S., for on 25 October 1950, the Chinese crossed the Yalu River and counterattacked south, defeating several South Korean and American units.

General MacArthur downplayed the Chinese presence, but still pressed for approval to bomb critical supply bridges along the Yalu River, something that President Truman still prohibited. Pressing the issue further, MacArthur passed reports to Washington stressing that the situation was becoming "increasingly critical" and the restrictions placed upon him by Washington were hampering his ability to stop the

---

[21] Ibid.

[22] Michael Pearlman, *Truman and MacArthur: Policy, Politics, and the Hunger for Honor and Renown* (Bloomington: Indiana University Press, 2008), 119.

[23] Herspring, *The Pentagon and the Presidency,* 78.

Chinese advance.[24] General MacArthur appealed to others stateside as well--sending simultaneous messages to numerous U.S. media outlets stating that Washington's micromanagement and restrictions had placed U.N. forces under "an enormous handicap, without precedent in military history."[25] Obviously, this infuriated President Truman, who subsequently issued guidance prohibiting all military commanders from dealing directly with any media outlets.[26]

As the relationship between President Truman and General MacArthur continued to deteriorate, so too did the situation in Korea. In December, Washington sent word to General MacArthur that no additional troops would be sent to Korea and the strategy would now become one to "defend successive positions," effectively limiting the scope of the conflict and ensuring it would not escalate any further.[27] President Truman and the Joint Chiefs knew how General MacArthur would take the news--General Bradley said:

> That night I thought long and hard. Truman, as president and commander-in-chief, had established our policy for the conduct of the Korean War. MacArthur was clearly opposed to that policy and had openly and defiantly challenged it to the point where there was a serious question that he would carry out that policy.[28]

Indeed General MacArthur was not happy with Washington's strategy. He responded to the Joint Chiefs that, "President Truman's resolute determination to free and unify that threatened land had now deteriorated almost into defeatism."[29] Still defiant and contemptuous of orders, MacArthur continued to lobby the Joint Chiefs to lift restrictions and change the policy. His unwavering attitude all by shattered any

---

[24] Ibid., 79.
[25] Ibid.
[26] Ibid., 80.
[27] Ibid.
[28] Omar Bradley and Clay Blair, *A General's Life: An Autobiography by General of the Army* (New York: Simon and Schuster, 1983), 634.
[29] Herspring, *The Pentagon and the Presidency,* 80.

relationship he had with the Chiefs, whom General MacArthur thought of as bureaucrats lacking the guts to take action.[30]

In a last ditch effort to gain support for his perceived "winning policy," MacArthur disregarded the President's direct order and contacted the United Press for an interview on 15 March 1951, and once again publicly condemned Truman's Korea policy. He followed on 24 March with a "military appraisal" of the situation in Korea, stating that the military strategy Washington directed hamstrung and undermined the efforts to get peace negotiations started with the Chinese and Korea.[31] Also made public during this time, was a letter General MacArthur had written earlier to Congressman Joe Martin, House Republican Leader, who had earlier directly solicited MacArthur's views on the Korean War.[32] In the letter, MacArthur had agreed with Martin's aggressive strategy to back Chinese Nationalists and allow them to invade China, and ended with his now famous quote, "There is no substitute for victory."[33] President Truman would later say that General MacArthur's letter "showed that the general was not only in disagreement with the policy of the government but was challenging this policy in open insubordination to his Commander-in-Chief."[34] For President Truman, this was the last straw, "By this act, MacArthur left me no choice--I [Truman] could no longer tolerate his insubordination."[35]

President Truman soon called a meeting with the Joint Chiefs and gained the unanimous recommendation that General MacArthur be relieved of command.[36] During

---

[30] Previdi, *Civilian Control Versus Military Rule*, 56.
[31] Herspring, *The Pentagon and the Presidency*, 81.
[32] Ibid.
[33] Ibid.
[34] Ibid.
[35] Truman, *Memoirs: Years of Trial and Hope*, 442.
[36] Herspring, *The Pentagon and the Presidency*, 82.

the discussion, General Bradley offered three supporting arguments in favor of relieving

General MacArthur, "First, the general's official communications and public statements

indicated a lack of sympathy with the limited war policy in Korea; second, MacArthur

had clearly violated the President's directive relative to public statements; third, The Joint

Chiefs of Staff, have felt and feel now, that the military *must be controlled by civilian

authority in this country.*"[37] Secretary of State Dean Acheson would later summarize the

situation, "We had the clearest idea among ourselves of the utter madness and folly of

what MacArthur was doing north. We sat around like paralyzed rabbits while MacArthur

carried out this nightmare…not one of us, myself prominently included, served [the

president] as he was entitled to be served."[38] In a Senate hearing following his firing,

General MacArthur stated:

> The general definition which for many decades has been accepted was that
> war was the ultimate process of politics; that when all other political
> means failed, you then go to force; and that when you do that, the balance
> of control…the minute you reach the killing stage, is the control of the
> military. A theater commander, in any campaign, is not merely limited to
> a handling of his troops; he commands that whole area politically,
> economically and militarily. You have got to trust at the stage of the game
> when politics fail, and the military takes over, you must trust the
> military.[39]

Certainly, this statement speaks volumes as to the skewed perspective MacArthur

had with respect to the civil-military relationship and the role senior military leaders have

in executing national policy. While MacArthur apparently viewed himself to be an

expert in carrying out "politics by other means," he saw virtually no connection or

relevance to any overriding policy (which he viewed to have failed at that point) that

---

[37] Ibid. (emphasis in original)

[38] Walter Isaacson and Evan Thomas, *The Wise Men: Six Friends and the World They Made* (New York: The Free Press, 1986), 251, quoted in Previdi, *Civilian Control Versus Military Rule*, 60.

[39] Henry Kissinger, Diplomacy (New York: Simon and Schuster, 1994), 485, quoted in Previdi, *Civilian Control Versus Military Rule*, 60.

resulted in military action. Rather than acting as an extension of that policy, MacArthur

viewed himself as the military expert that would now accomplish what earlier policy had

failed to do (securing the Korean peninsula), and would do so on his own terms. In an

even more telling exchange, when speaking to the Massachusetts General Court in July of

1951, MacArthur demonstrated that he indeed did not, in any respect, find himself or the

military subordinate to civilian control when he remarked:

> I find in existence a new and heretofore unknown and dangerous concept
> that the members of the armed forces owe their primary allegiance and
> loyalty to those who temporarily exercise the authority of the executive
> branch of the government, rather than to the country and its Constitution
> they are sworn to defend. No proposition could be more dangerous. None
> could cast greater doubt on the integrity of the Armed Forces.[40]

In short, General MacArthur found it a "dangerous concept" that career military

leaders like himself would take direction from "novice" (what he called temporary)

civilian leaders when it became necessary to employ military force. When summoned,

General MacArthur viewed his military expertise intrinsically superior to, and

superseding any civilian guidance or authority; moreover, he viewed this assertion as his

"duty" and what was in fact "demanded of him" under the Constitution he swore to

defend.

After relieving MacArthur, Truman appointed General Matthew Ridgway, who at

the time was commanding the 8th U.S. Army in Korea, to lead all United Nations Forces.

Although Ridgway admired MacArthur's military abilities, he did not agree with General

MacArthur's assertion that military officers draw their duty and allegiance from the

Constitution they are sworn to defend, rather than from the civilian leadership and

---

[40] Matthew Ridgway, *The Korean War* (Garden City: Doubleday, 1967), 233.

policies that the military is called upon to enforce.[41] In his memoir, Ridgway

commented:

> The concept of duty, in military service, has been elevated to extreme
> importance, and obedience to properly constituted authority is primal. No
> man in uniform, be he private or five-star general, may decide for himself
> whether an order is consonant with his personal views. While the loyalty
> he owes his superiors is reciprocated with equal force in the loyalty owed
> him from above, the authority of his superiors is not open to question.[42]

General Ridgway would go on to achieve "victory" by driving the Chinese out of

South Korea, and slowly paving the way for an Armistice in 1953 that put an end to the

military conflict. Certainly, Ridgway's criticism of MacArthur's views is consistent with

the "norm" and the general understanding of the American civil-military relationship.

Carl von Clausewitz agreed with, and summed up General Ridgway's critique of General

MacArthur's views in another way: "Subordinating the political point of view to the

military world would be absurd, for it is policy that has created war. Policy is the guiding

intelligence and war only the instrument, not vice versa. No other possibility exists, then,

than to subordinate the military point of view to the political.[43]

Vietnam

The case study of the Korean War demonstrates the potential for civil-military

conflict when the military assumes too much autonomy and takes actions that diverge

from the civilian authority's intent. The case study on the Vietnam War, however,

highlights the effects when that civil-military balance is tipped the other way, with the

---

[41] Herspring, *The Pentagon and the Presidency,* 82.
[42] Ridgway, *The Korean War*, 234.
[43] Carl von Clausewitz, *On War*, edited and translated by Michael Howard and Peter Paret. (Princeton: Princeton University Press, 1976), 733.

civilian leadership discounting military expertise and limiting any degree of military autonomy, resulting again in an unsynchronized political-military effort.

President Lyndon Johnson inherited the Vietnam War following President John Kennedy's assassination in 1963. From the day he took office, Johnson made it clear that he wanted any U.S. involvement in Vietnam to be limited, placing his plans to build the "Great Society" to conquer poverty and racial inequality at the forefront of his administration.[44] President Kennedy, due to his keen abilities and political savvy, had left behind a "loose" and unstructured policy system, which was unsuited for President Johnson's needs and did not serve him or the Administration well.[45] Due to the unstructured environment in the White House, much of the policy discussions and deliberations regarding the situation in Vietnam were often ad-hoc and excluded any military officers. Secretary of Defense Robert McNamara was a trusted Johnson advisor whose attendance at these meetings, the President felt, represented the views and advice of the military. Obviously, this situation did not sit well with the Joint Chiefs, who felt that without a direct audience to the President their advice and opinions were largely discounted and ignored. It was well known that President Johnson disliked any opinion that did not align with his own, which fueled his desire to surround himself with only those he trusted and knew would support his position and decisions. As Johnson's biographer noted, "Under siege…[Johnson's] operational style closed in and insulated him in the White House, where discussion was confined to those who offered no disagreement."[46] Johnson saw himself as the *formulator* of policy, and the National

---

[44] Herspring, *The Pentagon and the Presidency,* 152.
[45] Ibid., 151.
[46] Doris Kearns, *Lyndon Johnson and the American Dream* (New York: Harper and Row, 1976), 318.

45

Security Council, which under Eisenhower tended to develop policy options, as the *implementer* of presidential policy decisions.[47]

From the time Johnson took office, he and his administration struggled with defining a clear policy and strategy in Vietnam. For the most part, President Johnson trusted and empowered Secretary McNamara with the Vietnam War effort. Rather than settling on an overall strategy and seeking the advice of his military experts on how to best carry it out, Secretary McNamara instead formulated his own approach, one he thought to be consistent with the President's preferences. Secretary McNamara would settle on a strategy of "graduated response," where the U.S. would slowly ramp up offensive operations that would over time, demonstrate U.S. resolve and the futility of the North Vietnamese efforts. While this strategy appeased President Johnson's aim to limit the conflict in Vietnam and not impact his domestic agenda, the Joint Chiefs were strongly opposed to any murky strategy that would limit the full potential of the military and drag out the conflict.[48] The Chiefs' concerns about the growing complexity in Vietnam and the ramifications of such a strategy would fall on deaf ears. With his strategy approved by President Johnson, Secretary McNamara would now focus on implementation and how to best "quantify" the military's effectiveness of his policy.

Secretary McNamara's background as the youngest and first non-Ford CEO at the Ford Motor Company influenced his views on gauging success. As military leaders struggled to implement the strategy, Secretary McNamara focused on how to best "quantify" and measure its success. Drawing upon his success in the auto industry, and showing his naivety for the complexity of the situation in Vietnam, Secretary McNamara

---

[47] Herspring, *The Pentagon and the Presidency*, 151-152.
[48] Ibid.

decided that "body counts" of North Vietnamese Army (NVA) soldiers killed in action would best measure the success of his slow attrition strategy. General Westmoreland, the Commander of the Military Assistance Command, Vietnam (MACV), although wary of the policy, believed the "search and destroy" tactics and the resultant body count metrics he was required to report to Secretary McNamara would be in essence, the only way to "operationalize" such a strategy.[49] As the strategy continued, Secretary McNamara's civilian "CEO" approach and micromanagement continued to focus on metrics, which the Joint Chiefs and military commanders in the field had a difficult time executing and reporting. In a telling request, McNamara passed an order to Westmoreland to, "increase the percentage of VC/NVA base areas denied to Viet Cong from 10-20% to 40-50%," and to, "increase population in secure areas from 50 to 60%."[50] To the Joint Chiefs and military leaders in the field, such requests underscored the perceived failure of the Secretary and the President to understand and appreciate the reality of the situation in Vietnam, which was much more complex than managing the assembly floor at the Ford plant. Removing any doubt that Secretary McNamara and his approach lacked an appreciation for the complexity of what was unfolding in Vietnam, it was noted that after an update briefing at the American Pacific Headquarters in Honolulu, Secretary McNamara asked, "Now General, show me a graph that will tell me whether we are winning or losing in Vietnam."[51]

It was clear that in order to compensate for the lack of a sound and well defined policy in Vietnam, both the Secretary and President became involved in intrusive

---

[49] Ibid., 154. For an in-depth study on Westmoreland's views, see Samuel Zaffiri, *Westmoreland: A Biography of General William C. Westmoreland* (New York: Hearst Books, 1995).
[50] Ibid., 155.
[51] Previdi, *Civilian Control Versus Military Rule*, 96.

monitoring and meddling in military tactics.[52] The constant micromanagement and restrictions placed on military efforts continued to erode trust between the military and the civilian leadership. The Joint Chiefs continuously pressed for greater autonomy and an escalation in military action in North Vietnam, something they viewed as crucial to the war effort. Certainly, strikes to NVA supply lines along the Ho Chi Mihn Trail would weaken the NVA effectiveness in the south. However, both President Johnson and Secretary McNamara were weary of such a plan and believed that if the Joint Chiefs were given too much latitude for action, the war would "escalate" into a situation divergent from the Administration's limited war aims. In an open display of dissent, General Wallace Greene, the Commandant of the Marine Corps, began to visit military staff colleges voicing his concerns over the poor strategy in Vietnam and the lack of military consultation.[53] With such overt overwhelming dissent and continued disagreement from the Joint Chiefs, Secretary McNamara would cut off all direct military communication to the President, ensuring he retained a stronghold to policy recommendations to the White House.[54] Without direct access, the President's view of the purely military advice was subject to Secretary McNamara's skewed representation, which continued to deteriorate.

In February of 1965, the NVA began to escalate its intensity and launched a major attack on an American base killing eight soldiers.[55] Again, disagreement arose between the civilian and military leadership as to the appropriate action. While both civilian and military leaders favored a retaliatory strike, disagreements on the magnitude of such a strike divided the discussion. While the civilians still favored smaller "selective" targets

---

[52] Ibid., 88.
[53] Herspring, *The Pentagon and the Presidency,* 157.
[54] Ibid., 159.
[55] Ibid., 164.

that would "send a message" as to U.S. resolve, the Joint Chiefs favored a more intense

effort designed at leveraging mass and surprise in the North--the only way they thought

would effectively achieve the President's intent to demonstrate U.S. resolve and thwart

further North Vietnamese aggression. This issue would again divide the civilian and

military camps--the civilians believed such a military strategy was naïve and argued that,

"limited goals were best achieved using limited means."[56] The agreed upon retaliatory

effort, code named "Operation Rolling Thunder," would order selective air strikes under

the continued control and watchful eye of Washington. As the restrictive air operations

continued, it was apparent its effects had limited impact. As the situation continued to

deteriorate, military leaders called for increasing ground troops and intensifying the air

campaign. After a visit to evaluate the situation, the Army Chief of Staff, General Harold

Johnson reported to President Johnson that he estimated "up to 500,000 troops and five

years would be required to win the war."[57] General Johnson's observations and

recommendations would indeed come as a shock to Secretary McNamara and President

Johnson.

Understanding the current policy was flawed, and in a break from the "norm,"

President Johnson began to meet directly with the Joint Chiefs to gain their support. In

the end, and per their recommendations, he granted their request for additional troops and

would agree to loosen air strike restrictions, giving the military more autonomy. While

the President had loosened the reins slightly, McNamara held to the "graduated response"

strategy and continued to manage the war effort tightly. After Johnson approved a force

level increase from 82,000 to 175,000 in July of 1965, the Chiefs believed they were

---

[56] Ibid., 165.

[57] Robert S. McNamara, *In Retrospect: The Tragedy and Lessons of Vietnam* (New York: Vintage, 1995), 177.

making headway and continued to press the President for authorization to strike North Vietnamese infrastructure. This continued pressure would again put the Chiefs at odds with the President's strategy and would not serve the civil-military relationship well. At a meeting that took place in the Oval Office in November of 1965, where the Chiefs proposed intensifying the campaign, President Johnson screamed that "he was not going to let some military idiots talk him into World War III," then ordering the Chiefs "the get the hell out of his office."[58] While the civil-military relationship lingered at a low point, the graduated war of attrition continued with mediocre success. With limited options and a failing policy, Secretary McNamara would submit to the President in December of 1966 that he had grown "more and more convinced that we ought definitely to think of some action other than military action as the only program."[59]

Despite additional troop increases that now placed 470,000 Americans in Vietnam, the NVA and VC continued to pose significant opposition. The U.S. struggle to achieve "victory" had become a major issue for the American public as well as Congress, which felt hoodwinked by Johnson into authorizing the Gulf of Tonkin Resolution. At a Senate hearing regarding Rolling Thunder in August of 1967, the Joint Chiefs remarked that poor strategy and civilian interference inhibited the U.S. from achieving victory. The Chiefs argued that the only way to achieve victory was to disable NVA supply lines that supported the insurgency in the South.[60] Underscoring the complete disconnect between the civilian and military leadership, Secretary McNamara stringently rebutted the Joint Chiefs' position in front of the Senate. He argued that his strategy was indeed having an

---

[58] Lewis Sorley, *Honorable Warrior: General Harold Johnson and the Ethics of Command* (Lawrence: University Press of Kansas, 1998), 223.
[59] McNamara, *In Retrospect: The Tragedy and Lessons of Vietnam*, 223.
[60] Herspring, *The Pentagon and the Presidency*, 175.

effect on the enemy, and in essence, was winning the war in Vietnam.[61] Following the

hearing, the Joint Chiefs met and considered resigning in mass, but considered such an

act of "mutiny" potentially more harmful than what the current relationship produced.

There was also fallout from the Senate, which sided with the Joint Chiefs' position that

the graduated policy was ineffective and scorning civilian leadership for not considering

what they felt to be sound military advice. Following the release of the Senate report

detailing the account, President Johnson approved almost all of the military-proposed

targets that Secretary McNamara had previously prohibited. By late 1967, it was

apparent President Johnson had lost confidence in Secretary McNamara.[62]

The Tet Offensive in January of 1968, a massive full-scale attack by the NVA and

Viet Cong (VC), caught the U.S. by surprise and once again demonstrated North

Vietnamese determination and will. While the U.S. was able to thwart and attrit the

enemy over time, it once again highlighted the NVA's ability to seize the initiative and

maneuver offensively. President Johnson was left with limited options--he announced

that Secretary McNamara would retire and be replaced by Clark Clifford, who had served

on the Foreign Intelligence Advisory Board and as White House Council. Once

Secretary Clifford took over, President Johnson asked that he proceed with a full-scale

review of U.S. policy in Vietnam.[63] The Joint Chiefs found Secretary Clifford's

demeanor in stark contrast to McNamara's behavior. Clifford seemed to value their

inputs and respect the military expertise they were charged to provide. As the review

unfolded, the lack of strategy and policy became all too apparent. When asked to provide

---

[61] Mark Perry, *Four Stars: The Inside Story of the Forty-Year Battle Between the Joint Chiefs of Staff and America's Civilian Leaders* (Boston: Houghton Mifflin, 1989), 161-162.

[62] Herspring, *The Pentagon and the Presidency*, 176-177.

[63] Ibid.

specifics as to the amount of personnel needed and how they would be used to achieve

victory, the Chiefs were unable to do so. As Secretary Clifford put it,

> The military was utterly unable to provide an acceptable rationale for the troop increases. Moreover, when I asked for a presentation on their plan for attaining victory, I was told there was no plan for victory in the historic American sense. If blame had to be assessed, it lay with the president and his civilian advisors in the State Department and OSD. It was the civilian advisors who had convinced the president of the feasibility of carrying out a limited war, it was the civilians who had sold him on "gradualism;" and it was the civilians who through the President, placed the United States forces on the strategic defensive--a "no win" concept.[64]

Following the review, the U.S. would begin to adopt a strategy of

"Vietnamization" that would place more of an emphasis on supporting Vietnamese

efforts, and over time, slowly disengage the U.S. from the conflict. With U.S. negative

sentiment toward the war at an all-time high, a battered and beaten President Johnson

announced that he would not seek reelection for an additional term. In 1969, President

Johnson left office and handed the remainder of what was left of America's Vietnam War

strategy to President Nixon. Almost 30 years would pass before the Pentagon

experienced another dose of heavy-handed, disdainful leadership.

Afghanistan and Iraq

The inauguration of President George W. Bush in 2001 was seen by the military

establishment as a welcomed change. After providing murky policy direction and

indecision in Somalia, Bosnia, and Kosovo, coupled with his personal indiscretions and

convoluted stance on homosexuals in the military, his predecessor, President William

Jefferson Clinton, had developed a poor track record with the Joint Chiefs and the

military as a whole. President Bush appointed Donald Rumsfeld as the Secretary of

---

[64] Clark Clifford, *Counsel to the President* (New York: Random House, 1991), 493-94.

Defense, a position Secretary Rumsfeld previously held in the 1970s under the Ford administration. Secretary Rumsfeld immediately began to focus on transforming and strengthening the U.S. military, which he felt had been weakened by the Clinton administration.[65] Secretary Rumsfeld's transformation centered on moving away from large military force constructs designed for outdated conventional threats and toward a lighter and more mobile military that would leverage technology and airpower--a force he believed would be better suited to meet the unconventional threats of the future. He also believed that the civilian control of the military had eroded during the Clinton years, something he wanted to regain and reassert.[66] As Secretary Rumsfeld began to implement his changes, it became clear he was not interested in the input from the military Services--those that openly disagreed with his changes were pushed aside or dismissed. As one author commented, "The only individuals whose careers would survive and prosper were officers who were prepared to play Rumsfeld's game."[67]

In contrast to President Clinton's late-night policy discussions, President Bush's corporate background shaped his leadership style. From the beginning, President Bush let his administration know that he was not one to be involved in details and would rely on those with the expertise to provide answers to his questions.[68] This allowed the agencies and departments a great degree of autonomy to develop options and provide the President with recommendations. As President Bush empowered and delegated authority to his subordinates, elements within the U.S. government became a breeding ground for conflict and disagreement as department heads struggled for power. It would also allow

---

[65] Herspring, *The Pentagon and the Presidency,* 377.
[66] Ibid., 381.
[67] Ibid., 378.
[68] Ibid.

Secretary Rumsfeld and his controlling personality to dominate the formulation of national security policy completely.[69]

Although President Bush stated he would rely on the advice of the Joint Chiefs and other organizations like the CIA in military matters, Secretary Rumsfeld made it clear that those inputs would come through him and he would decide, regardless of Goldwater-Nichols,[70] if and when the Joint Chiefs would advise the President, for "he was convinced that he understood the national security problems facing the U.S. military better than the Chiefs."[71] Secretary Rumsfeld's mistrust of the military led to him work issues primarily with his civilian staff, avoiding the military if at all possible. Secretary Rumsfeld's caustic attitude toward the military was shared and perpetuated within the civilian staff:

> Working with a close-nit group, mostly civilians, he [Secretary Rumsfeld] was a mystery to many in the building, especially members of the Joint Chiefs of Staff, the uniformed heads of the Army, Navy, Air Force and Marine Corps. And these civilians shared his lack of respect for the uniformed military. Their attitude bordered on disdain, many officers thought. Snide comments slipped out frequently, 'You are all screwed up here,' or 'You screwed up there.' Never 'we'--the divide was always there.[72]

General Hugh Shelton, the Chairman of the JCS at the time, challenged Secretary Rumsfeld on many of his transformation policies. Shelton also objected to Rumsfeld's requirement to vet all visits and discussion points with him prior to advising the President on any matters--something he viewed to be at odds with his statutory responsibility to

---

[69] Ibid.

[70] Under The Goldwater-Nichols Department of Defense Reorganization Act of 1986, the Chairman of the Joint Chiefs of Staff was named the "principal military adviser to the President, the National Security Council, and the Secretary of Defense." For additional information, see *Goldwater-Nichols Department of Defense Reorganization Act of 1986*, H.R. 3622, 99th Cong., 2nd sess., Public Law 99-824 (October 1, 1986).

[71] Ibid.

[72] Dana Priest, *The Mission: Waging War and Keeping Peace with America's Military* (New York: Norton, 2003), 24.

advise the President directly. General Shelton's views obviously did not sit well with Secretary Rumsfeld, and would further degrade an already strained relationship with the Joint Chiefs, disenfranchising them completely from Secretary Rumsfeld's inner circle. Soon thereafter, General Shelton announced his retirement and the President appointed General Richard Meyers as his replacement, effective 1 October 2001. It was noted by an anonymous General familiar with the process, that the appointment of General Meyers "made it clear that the administration wanted obedience, not officers who might make waves."[73] It was also clear that the relationship between General Meyers and Rumsfeld was a marked improvement over that with General Shelton--General Meyers shared many of Rumsfeld's views and preferences, and for that reason, was given more latitude and access to Rumsfeld's "domain."

The attacks of 11 September 2001 would put Secretary Rumsfeld's plan to transform the military on hold, and would test the effectiveness of his leadership style and strained relationship with senior military officials. From the beginning, President Bush was keenly interested in what near-term military action the U.S. could take. General Franks, the USCENTCOM Commander, advised Secretary Rumsfeld that due to the complexity of the terrain and the asymmetric threat al Qaeda presented, it would take months to get enough forces into the area to operate effectively. Not happy with the response, and understanding that President Bush wanted immediate action, Secretary Rumsfeld told General Franks to "try again."[74]

On a meeting held on 12 September 2001 to discuss options for the 9/11 attacks, both Secretary Rumsfeld and his deputy, Paul Wolfowitz suggested that in addition to

---

[73] Herspring, *The Pentagon and the Presidency*, 383.
[74] Bob Woodward, *Bush at War* (New York: Simon and Schuster, 2002), 44.

attacking al Qaeda in Afghanistan, the President should consider options in Iraq as well.[75] Without a clear strategy for the military to carry out in Afghanistan, General Shelton voiced his opposition to such a plan unless Iraq could be tied to the 9/11 attacks.[76] Throughout the discussion, Secretary of State Colin Powell, General Shelton, and the President remained opposed to beginning any action in Iraq, believing that it would potentially ignite increased Middle Eastern dissent. Despite the President's opposition, Mr. Wolfowitz remained committed for U.S. action in Iraq, proposing such strikes as "the principal target of the first round in the war on terrorism."[77] President Bush decided to table the discussion on Iraq for the moment, and focus the team on "a real plan that would inflict real pain and destruction on the terrorists."[78]

After being presented with options for offensive action in Afghanistan, President Bush decided on a course of action that would entail the use of missile and air strikes, combined with a small amount of Special Forces troops in country.[79] With an overall concept chosen (despite any overall cohesive strategy), military planners still struggled to identify suitable "hard targets" in a country that was not at all industrialized and inhabited by an elusive and mobile enemy. On 2 October 2001, a frustrated Secretary Rumsfeld passed down an order detailing an overall strategy in a document entitled "Campaign against Terrorism: Strategic Guidance for the Department of Defense."[80] In it, Secretary Rumsfeld summarized *his* interpretation of what President Bush envisioned for the "War on Terrorism," explaining that the U.S. would not only target al Qaeda, but all other

---

[75] Ibid., 49.
[76] Herspring, *The Pentagon and the Presidency*, 385.
[77] Woodward, *Bush at War*, 49.
[78] Ibid.
[79] Herspring, *The Pentagon and the Presidency*, 386.
[80] Woodward, *Bush at War*, 189.

factions supporting or harboring terrorists, to include operations in multiple theaters.[81] Hastily, the military put together a target list consisting primarily of Taliban air defense systems and any groups of al Qaeda that could be located.[82] After gaining approval from the President on 7 October 2001, the U.S. began air strikes. As pilots and military planners struggled to locate and strike "meaningful" targets, it soon became clear that the overwhelming success that air power achieved in Operation Desert Storm, would remain elusive in Afghanistan.

As the operation continued, discussions surrounding the "transition" finally arose. Both President Bush and Secretary Rumsfeld were against "peacekeeping operations," with President Bush suggesting the U.S. "should attempt to bring in a U.N. protective force and then leave."[83] Just a month after U.S. offensive operations had commenced, ongoing air strikes and special operations teams meticulously struck al Qaeda and Taliban strongholds, leading General Meyers to report to the Secretary and the President that the Northern Alliance was now in control of more than half the country, with remnants of al Qaeda and the Taliban fleeing for the Pakistan border.[84] It appeared to all that although hastily planned, the U.S. would enjoy a quick military victory in Afghanistan, with only the simple task of the transition to a suitable Afghan security force and government remaining.

With the war in Afghanistan still underway, talks again centered on what to do in Iraq. The U.S. remained convinced that Saddam Hussein still had weapons of mass destruction (WMD) in his possession and continued to press for inspections that would

---

[81] Ibid.
[82] Herspring, *The Pentagon and the Presidency*, 386.
[83] Ibid., 388.
[84] Woodward, *Bush at War*, 312.

verify this assertion. With Hussein refusing inspections, and the 9/11 attacks still fresh in everyone's memory, many believed his regime posed a significant threat to America. From the beginning, Secretary Rumsfeld and his Deputy, Paul Wolfowitz, argued that the previous Bush Administration had made a mistake in not removing Hussein from power and that action had to be taken in Iraq to remove him from power now.[85] With President Bush in the middle, Secretary Rumsfeld and Vice President Cheney both pushed for a military option, while Secretary of State Colin Powell advocated for more of a diplomatic route, arguing that "containment" could still create regime change and would avoid any Middle East destabilization that a U.S. military operation may cause.[86]

Armed with Congressional approval for military action in Iraq, and following his State of the Union address citing Iraq as one of the "Axis of Evil" in January of 2002, President Bush gave the go ahead to Secretary Rumsfeld to begin detailed planning for Iraq.[87] Due to his already strained relationship with the Joint Chiefs, Secretary Rumsfeld went around the Chiefs and worked directly with General Franks on the development of a plan for Iraq.[88] Secretary Rumsfeld held firm on his idea of a smaller and more mobile force that would leverage technology, while General Franks advocated "The Powell Doctrine" approach that would employ a large and overwhelming force to defeat the enemy quickly.[89] This would remain a point of contention between the two during the planning phase. In February of 2002, President Bush signed a National Security Council directive laying out the goals and objectives for the war with Iraq, which Secretary

---

[85] Herspring, *The Pentagon and the Presidency*, 398.
[86] Woodward, *Bush at War*, 344-351.
[87] Herspring, *The Pentagon and the Presidency,* 398.
[88] Ibid.
[89] Bob Woodward, *Plan of Attack* (New York: Simon and Schuster, 2004), 80.

Rumsfeld and General Franks did not brief the Joint Chiefs on until March.[90] The Joint Chiefs were not happy that they had been kept in the dark; such actions highlighted the egotistical control that Secretary Rumsfeld maintained over the planning process.

As planning for the war in Iraq progressed, it was apparent that Secretary Rumsfeld would be involved in every detail of the process. With disagreement still existing with military leaders as to the size of the force, Secretary Rumsfeld maintained complete control over the process and would personally approve each unit slated for deployment. This resulted in a convoluted process that disrupted the military's planning system and hindered deployment efficiency, resulting in "taking 20 drafts of the battle plan [to the Secretary] to reconcile these contradictory impulses and produce a final strategy." [91] During this process, Rumsfeld and Franks continued to circumvent JCS involvement, and kept high-level planning and strategy discussions between themselves.[92] As the strategy unfolded, military leaders were still uneasy with the smaller force it called for, worried that the invasion force would become "…strung out, underprotected, and undersupplied."[93]

With the military plan taking shape, Secretary Rumsfeld turned his attention to how he would handle post-conflict Iraq. He wanted to ensure the reconstruction and political issues had been worked through, something he believed had been neglected in Bosnia. Secretary Rumsfeld remarked, "We do not want to be in a position where the failure of somebody to do those things ties our forces down indefinitely the way they

---

[90] Ibid., 118-119. See also Tommy Franks, *American Soldier* (New York: HarperCollins, 2004), 277-278.
[91] Herspring, *The Pentagon and the Presidency*, 400.
[92] Ibid.
[93] Ibid.

seem to be tied down in Bosnia indefinitely."[94] Secretary Rumsfeld believed that the Defense Department was better suited than the State Department to handle the planning and execution of the reconstruction phase, and appointed the Under Secretary of Policy, Douglas Feith to head up the effort, with General Franks and his military forces focusing only on security issues. Secretary Rumsfeld's orders were clear. He wanted "unity of effort and unity of leadership for the full range of reconstruction activities that need to be performed in order to say that mission is over and the troops can leave."[95] After the meeting with Secretary Rumsfeld that laid out these responsibilities, General Franks' deputy, Lt. General Renuart, remarked (with regard to the reconstruction responsibilities), "I think we just dodged a bullet," with General Franks replying, "Well you may be right. I have my marching orders. The secretary wants us to focus on security."[96] As the post-conflict planning effort went forward, friction grew between Mr. Feith's staff and the State Department. The State Department efforts to provide what they felt to be critical information on the post-conflict plan were often ignored, causing friction between Secretary Powell and Secretary Rumsfeld.[97]

In March of 2003, armed with information that Saddam Hussein indeed possessed WMD, President Bush gave the go ahead to commence with Secretary Rumsfeld's military plan. In the end, Secretary Rumsfeld's smaller force package was indeed successful, facing little opposition and defeating the Iraqi army in just over three weeks. It would become all too apparent that although the lighter force was well suited to advance quickly and defeat the Iraqi military forces, it was not at all right-sized to handle

---

[94] Bob Woodward, *State of Denial: Bush at War* (New York: Simon and Shuster Paperbacks, 2006), 91.
[95] Ibid.
[96] Ibid.
[97] Herspring, *The Pentagon and the Presidency*, 401.

the civil unrest and turbulence the post-conflict phase would present. As the U.S. continued to struggle with providing security amidst a growing insurgency, Secretary Rumsfeld looked past it all and viewed the quick military victory in Iraq as a vindication that his transformational ideas and strategy to employ smaller and more mobile forces had indeed proved successful.

Drawing Civil-Military Lessons

The case studies presented highlight three historic examples where the civil-military relationship was less than optimal. While all three case studies highlight varying degrees of friction and dysfunction within the relationship, all serve as examples of how the sub-optimization of the civil-military relationship can hinder the ability to harness and focus America's collective efforts to provide security for the nation and carry out national objectives. The case studies demonstrate such acrimony within the civil-military relationship can accrue collectively, or from individuals or dysfunction within the independent military or civilian spheres. Regardless of which side of the civil-military equation impedes collaboration--the recalcitrant military commander with no regard for civilian direction or a mistrusting civilian leader who meddles in military operational matters--both equally bear the burden and share the risk of hindering the harmonization of national efforts and pose a risk to national security. Gaining an appreciation for the background, context and relational interplay demonstrated within these case studies serves to educate rising senior military leaders, preparing them to better navigate and successfully manage the civil-military relationship they may find themselves engaged in the future.

The Korean War case study demonstrated how acute divergent preferences between General MacArthur and President Truman led to tremendous friction and unsynchronized efforts. Although President Truman's policy and strategy was to fight a limited war with North Korea to maintain the "status quo" between the north and the south, General MacArthur had his own ideas about which military strategy would best suit U.S. interests and vigorously pursued it. With ample reason, President Truman and the Chiefs believed General MacArthur would not carry out the declared strategy in good faith, therefore intrusively monitoring his actions and imposing restrictions to limit any dangerous "liberties" he may take in his military translation of President Truman's policy. Leveraging his "heroic celebrity" within society, he openly chastised the President's strategy in the media and appealed to members of Congress as an avenue to circumvent what he believed to be a "losing strategy" in Korea. Discounting the military's subordination to civil authority, MacArthur believed that in the case of Korea, civilian leaders did not indeed "have the right to be wrong," and insisted (and attempted to demonstrate) that his military expertise superseded the "misguided" strategy that President Truman had asked him to execute. While his actions were seen as an act of insubordination to the President, General MacArthur believed them to be subordinate to the Constitution and to the country he swore to defend--a higher calling that he believed eclipsed any perceived misguided civilian direction. In short, General MacArthur believed he was right and President Truman was wrong, and in every way "shirked" the duties President Truman gave him.

The complex situation in Vietnam and the "limited war" called for by President Johnson would again cause friction between the civilian and military spheres. This time however, the President and the Secretary of Defense would dominate and hinder the civil-military relationship. Without a clearly stated objective or strategy in Vietnam for the military to translate and execute, President Johnson and Secretary McNamara dominated the military sphere, providing limited autonomy to military leaders and excluding much of their input and potential expertise. The perceived lack of trust between military leaders and the President would scar the relationship for the duration of President Johnson's administration, limiting any potential success more collaborative efforts may have achieved in Vietnam. While military leaders made good faith efforts to offer sound expert advice on which military course of action they thought best represented the translation of the perceived strategy and policy into action, President Johnson and Secretary McNamara instead guided military operations through their perceived superior operational expertise. In the end, the dysfunction between the civilian and military spheres would present at the very least, an uncoordinated and hampered effort at any potential success the U.S. may have achieved in Vietnam. Certainly, given the complexities of the situation and the asymmetric threat the enemy presented, even a well thought out and collaborative effort may have still proved difficult under the circumstances. The stubborn approach and hubris exhibited by the civilian leadership stunted any potential synergy and inevitably doomed U.S. intentions in the country. In this case, the civilian authority's "right to be wrong" indeed painfully played out through the perspective of the military. As subordinate "experts in the management of violence," it is imperative that military leaders, in good faith, strive to ensure their expertise and input is presented rationally, and if necessary, vigorously, to avoid such pitfalls in the future. While civilians maintain the "right to be wrong," the aim of the military leader must then be the compelling presentation of sage military expertise that may give the civilian leader room to question such an assertion.

The events of 9/11 and the ensuing "War on Terrorism" is yet another example of a complex situation that would require the keen collaboration between both the military and civilian spheres to achieve success. While President Bush's "hands off" approach was favorable to the military, potential military autonomy and effectiveness was eclipsed by an overpowering Secretary of Defense, who often dominated the discussion and limited military input. President Bush's desire to formulate a quick response to the events of 9/11 caused friction between Secretary Rumsfeld and military leaders, as planners struggled to develop a comprehensive strategy and suitable targets against an elusive mobile enemy with limited targetable infrastructure. In the end, the lighter and more mobile force Secretary Rumsfeld pushed for would prove somewhat successful in the near term, but the lack of forces on the ground and the asymmetric tactics employed by al Qaeda in Iraq paved the way for an insurgency that has lasted years.

The decision to invade Iraq would cause additional friction between the military and civilian spheres. With an already strained relationship between Secretary Rumsfeld's staff and the military leaders in Washington, Secretary Rumsfeld elected to work directly with General Franks in formulating a strategy. While General Franks pushed for a larger force that would be better suited to handle all phases of the operation, Secretary Rumsfeld pushed again for a lighter force consistent with the "transformational" ideas he mandated at the beginning of his tenure as Secretary of Defense. The disagreement in strategy would cause Secretary Rumsfeld to monitor the military intrusively, ensuring he remained "intimately" involved with every operational and tactical detail. With the precedent of Secretary Rumsfeld's "decision autonomy" well-established, General Franks did not pose opposition when Secretary Rumsfeld decided to place his own staff in charge of the Iraq post-conflict reconstruction phase. Understanding the complexity and risks associated with this phase, General Franks viewed Secretary Rumsfeld's decision with "relief" rather than concern. While General Frank's actions may have constituted "working" by following orders and not questioning Rumsfeld's decision, he indeed "shirked" his greater duty as a military leader to responsibly convey his expert advice and judgment. Had the planning atmosphere been more collaborative between both the military and civilian spheres, the post-conflict phase may have been handled differently and more effectively. In the end, Secretary Rumsfeld's light force was effective against Iraq's military forces, but was not suited to handle the larger and more important task of stabilizing the post-war country--a task driven by poorly developed overall strategy and the product of a less than optimum civil-military relationship.

CHAPTER 3: THE CHALLENGE

The case studies presented highlight instances of increased friction and dysfunction between military leaders in post-World War II conflicts. This new era has presented, and will continue to present, complexities that will challenge U.S. resolve and call for focused efforts that effectively leverage all elements of U.S. power. While both Huntington and Janowitz framed the issue and offered models they believed explained and best optimized this critical relationship during the period of the Cold War, both theories seem to fall short when applied in the context of today's complex environment. Advantages of Huntington's idea of objective control and complete military autonomy may be well suited to the previous era's conventional engagements, but his prescribed military detachment from civilian policy and its formulation seem a hindrance in today's environment, where the military is increasingly engaged and charged with carrying out U.S. policy in complex environments like Iraq and Afghanistan. Conversely, Janowitz's assertion that the military becoming more "civilianized" and therefore inherently better "in-tune" with the policies and politics of the civilian leadership seems to fall too far on the other end of the spectrum, with the constabulary force he proposed potentially not meeting the spectrum of functional demands the nation's security requires. The question then, for rising senior military leaders in today's environment, is what pattern or model best serves the civil-military relationship and is best suited to address U.S. interests in the future?

Richard Kohn, a Professor of History and Peace, War, and Defense at the University of North Carolina at Chapel Hill, believes there is no "cookbook recipe" for civil-military relations that answers the question. He believes that as recent history has shown the friction between both spheres can and will continue arise due to "their differing needs, perspectives, and objectives in peacetime and in waging war."[1] He believes that optimizing this relationship does not come from "theory or structure of society," but from a trust fostered between both spheres that leverage personal relationships "at the highest levels of American Government." While this trust should rest on both sides of the equation, he believes that the burden ultimately falls on the shoulders of the military, stating:

> Senior military leaders have a professional duty to teach their civilian superiors and to shape the relationship, just as doctors do with their patients, lawyers with their clients, teachers with their students, and all professionals with those they serve. Officers are the long-term stewards of national security: they must think about and practice civil-military relations on a continuing basis, and recognize its study as necessary to fulfill their role in society effectively.[2]

Colonel Matthew Moten, a Professor and Deputy Head of the Department of History at the U.S. Military Academy, believes Huntington's model of objective control stands "at odds with human reality" and supports Professor Kohn's assertion that institutional structure aside, responsible dialog and trust at the highest levels is the only way to ensure that the development of military strategy is well-suited and appropriate to the policy it serves. As Colonel Moten put it,

> Implicit in it is the notion of a wall between strategy and policy: between the soldier's and the statesman's roles and duties. Try as each party might, however, maintaining that wall is impossible, given the nature of warfare, the seamlessness of policy and strategy, the Clausewitzan idea

---

[1] Richard H. Kohn, "Building Trust: Civil-Military Behaviors for Effective National Security," in *American Civil Military Relations: The Soldier and the State in a New Era*, Suzanne C. Nielsen and Don M. Snider (Baltimore: The Johns Hopkins University Press), 265.

[2] Ibid., 287.

that war is an extension of policy by other means, and the constitutional separation of war powers.[3]

Given the subordinate role of the military to civilian leadership, Colonel Moten points out that while each side may strive for equal footing and trust within the dialogue that shapes policy formulation, in the end, the military must appreciate the supremacy of the civilian's ultimate authority and stand ready to accept and execute the decisions they ultimately hand down. As Colonel Moten continues:

> Still, the idea that civil authority must dominate, even in matters of operational detail if civilians so choose, may be difficult for some officers to accept, for it demands a high level of professional maturity--self-abnegation, a tolerance for ambiguity, and a willingness to accept compromise between important but competing values. Yet it's the very essence of civilian control.[4]

The case studies contained in this paper indeed highlighted differing scales of a military leader's "willingness to accept compromise" that Colonel Moten asserts is critical to the relationship and function of civilian control. While General MacArthur's blatant disregard for President Truman's orders stand in stark contrast to General Franks' negligent submission to support Secretary Rumsfeld's plan to exclude the military from Phase IV planning in Iraq, both serve as irresponsible examples of a military leader's obligation and arrive far short of the ideal that both Professor Kohn and Colonel Moten suggest. While simple to label General MacArthur's actions during the Korean War as "insubordinate" and certainly not serving the civil-military relationship well, General Franks' actions, although not as overtly obvious, still stands in violation to his obligation. James Burk, a professor of sociology at Texas A&M University, labels such actions as

---

[3] Matthew Moten, "A Broken Dialogue: Rumsfeld, Shinseki, and Civil-Military Tension," in Nielsen and Snider, *American Civil Military Relations: The Soldier and the State in a New Era*, 69.
[4] Ibid., 70.

"thoughtless obedience," which he believes occurs "when public servants suspend their critical judgment about the good, which makes them available to serve unjust ends."[5]

Both Huntington and Janowitz discussed the influence of America's societal values on the military force and the potential impacts on "military professionalism." The repeal of the Clinton era's ambiguous "Don't ask, Don't tell" policy and new regulations allowing women to serve in combat roles from which they were previously excluded, serve as recent examples of the military slowly adopting and adhering to societal norms-- something Huntington argued would inevitably weaken the military's effectiveness and detract from the "military mind" that was cultivated by excluding such societal influences. Janowitz, conversely, believed such "civilianization" of the military would prove beneficial and limit friction generated by a military force with divergent values and ideologies than the society it protected. Certainly, it is too early to gauge the impact such military migration towards societal "norms" will produce. Reassessing the evolution of U.S. military professionalism, Major Darrell Driver, a former assistant professor of political science at West Point offered an appropriate intellectual compromise, commenting that "the professional ethic is best served not by searching for a comprehensive ideology in which all military professionals might share, but by recognition that military service is compatible with a broad range of political commitments."[6] Driver argues the professionalism and effectiveness abundant in the American military force is not a product of its separatist ideology, but rather is born from

---

[5] James Burk, "Responsible Obedience by Military Professionals: The Discretion to Do What is Wrong," in Nielsen and Snider, *American Civil Military Relations: The Soldier and the State in a New Era*, 155.

[6] Darrell W. Driver, "The Military Mind: A Reassessment of the Ideological Roots of American Military Professionalism," in Nielsen and Snider, *American Civil Military Relations: The Soldier and the State in a New Era*, 189.

the public service ethos and commitment embodied within the individuals that serve. As he puts it:

> The continued promulgation of the notion that the military professionals share some distinct and professionally necessary ideology that isolates-- and by some accounts elevates--military professionals is not empirically demonstrable, nor is it conductive to meeting the military-functional and democratic-societal demands of a twenty-first-century force. Instead of clarifying the military professional's duties and roles, attempts to locate a unique and separate military ideology have confused them.[7]

No matter where one falls on the spectrum from Huntington to Janowitz, all must agree that the health of American civil-military relations rests on the professionalism of both senior military officers and the nation's civilian leadership. After becoming familiar with the theorists and case studies presented in this paper, it is easy to agree with Professor Kohn that no single "cook book recipe" can adequately address the complexities and nuances of the civil-military relationship within the context of an ever rapidly changing strategic landscape. As we have seen, along with the crucial responsibilities and duties given to our senior military and civilian leaders, come strong personalities and convictions, which can indeed negatively impact the balance and collaborative effect if not managed properly. Fostering relationships and establishing trust between the two spheres will be critical to U.S. success and will be the charge of the rising senior military leader in the future.

---

[7] Ibid.

70

CHAPTER 4: CONCLUSION

Wherever democratic states face the challenge of providing for their own security, inevitably friction between military and civilian leaders concerning the ends, ways, and means of attaining that security will exist. The civil-military disconnects observed within the present administration as well as the historical examples presented in this thesis illustrate how America must strive to do better. To avoid such pitfalls in the future, it is crucial that our rising senior military leaders arrive prepared and armed with tools that will allow them to better engage in the civil-military dialogue and shape the level of collaboration that present-day and future strategic complexities demand.

As this paper has shown, civil-military disconnects frequently exist at the strategic and operational nexus--the very domain upon which the JAWS curriculum focuses. With the goal of the JAWS course to graduate senior joint officers proficient at translating broad strategic guidance into tangible operational plans, it seems logical to include additional curriculum that would provide JAWS students with a deeper understanding of civil-military relations and the manifold impact it has at the highest levels of strategic and policy planning.

The JAWS civil-military curriculum proposed by this thesis centers on the topics and their phasing contained within this paper. First, students must be exposed to the key civil-military relations theorists, such as Samuel Huntington and Morris Janowitz. In doing so, students will gain a deeper understanding of the broad range of areas that define and influence civil-military relations. Armed with a variety of theoretical frameworks, students should then examine a cross-section of present-day and historical case studies (like the ones presented here) that highlight civil-military friction and discuss the effect such friction had on U.S. national security. Finally, a panel or forum consisting of civil-military scholars and senior military and civilian leaders (active and/or retired) would serve as a capstone to the course and allow each panel member to share their respective thoughts on the issue and give students a chance to interact and ask questions relevant to the case studies reviewed. Armed with the knowledge gleaned from this course, JAWS graduates, as rising senior military leaders, will be better prepared to operate effectively in an increasingly complex environment that calls for and demands a new level of collaboration and synergy between the military and civilian spheres.

This Page Intentionally Blank

ANNOTATED BIBLIOGRAPHY

Books and Theses

Baral, Jaya Krishna. *The Pentagon and the Making of U.S. Foreign Policy*. Atlantic
        Highlands: Humanities Press, 1978.

Dr. Baral uses the three models presented by political scientist Graham T. Allison is his
book, *Essence of Decision*, to explore the formulation and implementation of U.S. foreign
policy and decision making. Using Vietnam as a case study, Dr. Baral examines how the
military and civilian spheres interacted, gaging whether the military "controlled" the
foreign policy process during this period, or acted merely as the "instrument"
implementing the civilian elite's interests. While Dr. Baral concedes the pendulum of
influence between the two spheres varied as the conflict escalated, he concluded that
during this period in general, the military did not dominate the process, nor did it act
solely as an instrument.

Clausewitz, Carl Von. *On War*. Indexed edition. Translated by Michael Howard and
        Peter Paret. Princeton: Princeton University Press, 1976.

Carl Von Clausewitz was a Prussian soldier and German military theorist. His most
notable work, *On War*, which was left unfinished upon his death in 1831, centers on the
theoretical, political, and human aspects of war. *On War* is well-suited to augment the
study of civil-military relations, in that he discounts any "scientific" approach to war, and
instead aims to educate the reader as to the intricacies and linkage between desired
political end states and the military objectives designed to achieve them. Clausewitz's
emphasis on the "human" element and the strategic role it plays make his work relevant
in today's complex strategic environment of "limited war." While the civil-military
relations theme is echoed throughout *On War*, Book Eight is well-suited to address the
civil-military challenge in terms of linking political aims with military objectives.

Clifford, Clark. *Counsel to the President*. New York: Random House, 1991.

Counsel to the President is Clark Clifford's autobiography detailing his time as Assistant
to the Naval Advisor to the President, White House Counsel to President Truman from
1944-1950, through his tenure as Secretary of Defense under the President Johnson
administration from 1968-1969. It provides a first-hand account of the policy
formulation in the years leading up to the Cold War as well as a personal account of
Clifford's privately disputed objections with President Johnson's policies in Vietnam.

Cohen, Eliot A. *Supreme Command*. New York: Anchor Books, 2003.

Eliot Cohen is a professor of Strategic Studies at Johns Hopkins University. He is a prior Army intelligence officer that served on the policy planning staff at the Office of Secretary of Defense. *Supreme Command* centers on the civil-military relationship between the civilian leaders and military commanders during times of war. Professor Cohen examines and analyzes the relationship and friction between four civilian statesmen (Lincoln, Clemenceau, Churchill, and Ben-Gurion) and the military leaders who served them in an effort to "uncover the nature of the strategy-making in war." After his case studies, he ends with an exceptional synopsis of civil-military theory and the idea of military professionalism, analyzing Huntington's "objective control" model and its applicability in the present-day environment. He concludes that the boundaries separating military means and political ends are more complex and uncertain than suggested by Huntington's "objective control" model. Cohen argues that for civilian control to be effective, the civil-military relationship must be a collaborative effort bound by trust that leverages the unique strengths and perspectives of each independent sphere.

Coles, Harry L, and Albert K. Weinberg. *Civil Affairs: Soldiers Become Governors*.
    Washington D.C.: U.S. Government Printing Office, 1964.

After major combat operations had ceased after World War II, the Army, charged with rehabilitating and reconstructing war-torn countries, struggled to move away from their traditional combat role and assume a more civil affairs-centric role. *Civil Affairs: Soldiers Become Governors* details how the Army came to grips with its new role, juggling national interests, interpreting policy and mitigating economic and financial problems while preserving cultural heritages. While the book was written in 1964, the issue of blurred lines separating military and civilian-centric activities in Phase IV operations remains relevant.

Desch, Michael C. *Civilian Control of the Military*. Baltimore: The Johns Hopkins
    University Press, 1999.

Civilian Control of the Military explores the issue of civilian control over the military and examines under what circumstances, wartime or peacetime, this control is maximized. Desch argues against Harold Lasswell's assertion that civilians can exert better control over the military during peacetime. Conversely, Desch asserts that civilian control is maximized and most effective under wartime periods, where civilian leadership is keenly interested and focused on military decision making and activities. To illustrate his position, he examines a broad spectrum of examples ranging from World Wars I and II, the Pre and post-Cold War era, and present day issues surrounding Latin America.

Feaver, Peter D. *Guarding the Guardians: Civilian Control of Nuclear Weapons in the United States*. Ithaca: Cornell University Press, 1992.

Centering on the post-Cold War era, Feaver examines the complexities surrounding command and control in the nuclear era, and the new dimension it brought to civil-military relations. Feaver examines the hierarchy of control from the President down to the military nuclear operators, highlighting the issues and constraints nuclear warfare presented to the civil-military relationship. Feaver ends with a historical study, examining the Truman, Eisenhower and Kennedy administrations and their respective accounts surrounding civilian control in the nuclear era.

-----. *Armed Servants*. Cambridge: Harvard University Press, 2003.

While Huntington and Janowitz offered theories describing what civil-military model they believed to be most effective, Feaver offers a model that he believes describes how the civil-military relationship actually plays out on a day-to-day basis. In Armed Servants, Feaver's "Agency Theory" examines the impact that divergent or aligned preferences between the civilian leadership (principal) and military (agent) has on civilian control. Feaver discusses intrusive and non-intrusive "control measures" civilians may elect to employ to ensure the military agent faithfully carries out the principal's intent (what Feaver calls "working"), rather than serve his own preferences (what Feaver labels "shirking").

Feaver, Peter D., and Christopher Gelpi. *Choosing Your Battles*. Princeton: Princeton University Press, 2004.

Feaver and Gelpi examine again the idea of an existing "civil-military gap" and the impact it may have on the formulation of American foreign policy. Citing historical examples, they examine the influence that prior military service plays on American civilian elites and the impact that service has on the propensity of civilian leaders to engage in military use of force. They conclude that civilians with prior military service are more inclined to engage the military against traditional "realpolitik" threats, but hesitant to become involved militarily in foreign humanitarian and "less-than-vital-interest" scenarios. Conversely, they found civilian leaders with no military background more apt to engage the military in wider, more "interventionalist" roles.

Feaver, Peter D, and Richard H. Kohn. *Soldiers and Civilians: The Civil-Military Gap and American National Security*. Cambridge: MIT Press, 2001.

Feaver and Kohn examine the perceived "gap" among the civilian and military spheres by dissecting and analyzing the relationship and interplay among civilian and military leaders. While the authors acknowledge varying degrees of lack of cooperation between the two spheres, they conclude that no civil-military crisis currently exists. However, they do highlight a perceived trend of senior military officers diverging from purely "advisor" roles with respect to policy and implementation, to more of an "insist" role, where military personal preferences skew advice and undermine the essence of the relationship.

Franks, Tommy. *American Soldier*. New York: HarperCollins, 2004.

This General Franks' autobiography details his time as Commander of USCENTCOM from 2000 to 2003. His personal account of the planning and decisions surrounding both wars in Iraq and Afghanistan provide details and paint a picture from his perspective on the personalities and the civil-military relationships that played out during this time frame.

Grynkewich, Alexus G. "The Airman and the State: An F-22 Pilot's Perspective on Civil-Military Relations." Masters Thesis, Joint Advanced Warfighting School, 2010.

Lt Col Grynkewich (USAF) presents a case study of the F-22 program, concluding that discourse between the civilian and military spheres resulted in a less-than-optimum fleet of F-22s. Labeling the "traditional" civil-military relations construct as the culprit, Grynkewich argues such traditional constructs must be replaced with a "collaborative norm," leading to more coherent strategies and successful outcomes in the future.

Goulden, Joseph C. Korea: *The Untold Story of the War*. New York: Times Books, 1982.

Leveraging [then] recently declassified and previously unpublished documents, *The Untold Story of the Korean War* was Goulden's attempt to capture "the big picture" surrounding the Korean War--something he felt had not yet been accomplished (as of 1982). Goulden's account of the Korean War is detailed and organized in a chronological manor that will enable the civil-military reader to quickly access chapters surrounding particular events or time periods. The book provides a great source for information and analysis surrounding the study of civil-military relations and the Korean War.

Haynes, Richard F. *The Awesome Power: Harry S. Truman as Commander in Chief.*
    Baton Rouge: Louisiana State University Press, 1973.

Haynes chronicles Truman's tenure as President of the United States and examines the context and circumstances surrounding his leadership and some of his most historic decisions; including Truman's decision to employ the atomic bomb on the Japanese and the firing of General MacArthur during the Korean War. While the book serves as an excellent historical record, Haynes detailed account paints a poignant picture of President Truman's demeanor and personality and the effect it had on his relationships and subsequent decision-making.

Herspring, Dale R. *The Pentagon and the Presidency: Civil-Military Relations From
    FDR to George W. Bush.* Lawrence: The University Press of Kansas, 2005.

Drawing from numerous sources, Herspring succinctly details and summarizes the civil-military relationship of 12 Presidents and their administrations, ranging from Franklin Roosevelt to George W. Bush. Herspring's case studies of Presidential administrations details and assesses the relationship with the military and its subsequent effectiveness with respect to security and civilian control. With the individual case studies serving as historic "civil-military relations markers," *The Pentagon and the Presidency* offers an account of how civil-military relations have evolved over the years, into what Herspring believes to be much more bureaucratic and politically-involved than in the past.

Higgins, Trumbull. *Korea and the Fall of MacArthur.* New York: Oxford University
    Press, 1960.

Higgins was a professor of history at John Jay College of Criminal Justice and the author of numerous books concerning the formulation of military policy and strategy. Korea and the Fall of MacArthur examines the events, the decisions, and policy formulation leading up to and during the Korean War. This book is organized into numerous chronological chapters, which make it easy for the civil-military reader to locate specific areas of interest pertaining to the Korean War. An excellent source that details civil-military relations and policy formulation during the Korean War.

Huntington, Samuel P. *The Soldier and the State: The Theory and Politics of Civil-Military Relations*. Cambridge: The Belknap Press of Harvard University Press, 1964.

Published in 1957, Samuel Huntington's *The Soldier and the State* was the first notable attempt to define and describe the phenomena of U.S. civil-military relations. Huntington proposes a theoretical framework that has been widely accepted as the foundation for the discussion of U.S. civil-military relations. Huntington's "Institutional Theory" explores his perception of diverging attitudes and values between what he viewed as the "conservative" military force and the "liberal" society it protected. Huntington's theory of "objective control" and his ideas surrounding military autonomy and professionalism offer a definite starting point for anyone interested in the study of civil-military relations.

Janowitz, Morris. *The Professional Soldier: A Social and Political Portrait*. New York: The Free Press, 1971.

Published after *The Soldier and the State*, Janowitz's "Convergence Theory" stands in contrast to Huntington's model. Janowitz viewed the post-World War II era and the ensuring Cold War with the Soviet Union driven largely by a new spectrum of warfare that would call for increased "convergence" between society, civilian leaders and the military, calling for a new type of security force--the "constabulary force." *The Professional Soldier* offers an opposing look (to that of Huntington's) at civil-military relations theory, and while published in 1971, still provides relevant arguments for today's environment.

Langston, Thomas S. *Uneasy Balance: Civil-Military Relations in Peacetime America Since 1783*. Baltimore: The John Hopkins University Press, 2003.

Uneasy Balance examines historic post-war eras and the ensuing priority "realignment" and civil-military relations that America dealt with in the transition from one war to the preparation for the next security threat. Langston explores periods from the Revolutionary War to the War in Iraq, evaluating the "balance" of relative power and influence between the civilian and military spheres surrounding post-war assessment and future planning. Langston argues America has a poor track record of achieving an effective post-war balance, and believes the current era (what he labels the "post-Cold War realignment") can still have a positive outcome if a greater level of collaboration and trust between both spheres is achieved.

Matthews, Colonel Lloyd J. *The Political-Military Rivalry for Operational Control in U.S. Military Actions: A Soldiers Perspective*. Carlisle: Strategic Studies Institute, 1998.

Colonel Matthew's Army War College monograph centers on emerging technology and its battlefield implications, giving NCA civilian authorities the ability to intervene below the strategic level. Citing case studies and examples, Matthews demonstrates how such civilian monitoring and intervention into military operational matters led to friction and unintended results. His short conclusion leveraging an "imaginary conversation" between a general and politician who are both Clausewitz scholars summarizes the strategic civil-military challenge and offers the author's solution.

McMaster, H.R. *Dereliction of Duty*. New York: HarperCollins, 1998.

As of 2011, H.R. McMaster was an Army Brigadier General and currently serving in the ISAF J5, Kabul, Afghanistan. As an active duty Army officer, McMaster brings a unique perspective in his work surrounding the decision-making and policy formulation during the Vietnam War. Leveraging recently declassified documents, McMaster sheds new light and insight into what he calls "one of the greatest American foreign policy disasters of the twentieth century."

McNamara, Robert S. *In Retrospect: The Tragedy and Lessons of Vietnam*. New York: Vintage, 1995.

In Retrospect is McNamara's personal account of his time serving both Presidents Kennedy and Johnson as the Secretary of Defense during the Vietnam War. Published in 1995, and 20 years after the Vietnam War, *In Retrospect* captures a personal and detailed look into the decisions and policymaking surrounding the conflict. Chapter 11, "The Lessons of Vietnam," is McNamara's short and concise description of how and why we failed in Vietnam, citing "11 major causes" centered on strategy and political-military planning, and bearing sharp relevance to current wars in Iraq and Afghanistan.

Millett, Allan R. *The American Political System and Civilian Control of the Military: A Historical Perspective*. Columbus: Mershon Center of the Ohio State University, 1979.

Millett examines the effectiveness of civilian control during three eras: The 19th century, World War II and in the 1970s. Millett offers relevant insight surrounding what civilian control of the military is supposed to accomplish and how that has played out within the American political system during those time periods. He concludes that civilian control of the military remained "functional" during his case studies, and any organizational "reform" to improve it has been eclipsed by the competing priorities of defense spending and resource allocation and their linkage to strategic diplomacy.

Nielsen, Suzanne C., and Don M. Snider. *American Civil-Military Relations: The Soldier and the State in a New Era.* Baltimore: The Johns Hopkins University Press, 2009.

A superb integration of individual essays from respected scholars examining many facets of the issues and ideas surrounding the present-day civil-military relations debate. The collection of essays shed new light and provide a "21st century perspective" on the very issues Samuel Huntington introduced back in 1957. Examining the civil-military relationship since the publishing of *The Soldier and the State*, the book investigates the present-day influence of Huntington's "societal and functional" imperatives, and frames the debate surrounding what civil-military relational "norm" is required to be effective in the current strategic environment. The work is a great resource that pools many respected authors thoughts together to synthesize the essence of today's civil-military relations debate.

Omar Bradley, and Clay Blair. *A General's Life: An Autobiography by General of the Army.* New York: Simon and Schuster, 1983.

An autobiography co-authored by Clay Blair detailing Bradley's service in the Army from 1915 through 1953. Serving as the very first Joint Chief of Staff and the last General to hold the rank of "Five Star General," Bradley's *A General's Life* provides the civil-military relations student with a unique perspective on both World War II and the Korean War. Of particular interest is his testimony during the Korean War as the first Joint Chief, and his personal account of the issues surrounding the firing of General MacArthur. Bradley died prior to the book's completion, leaving Blair to complete it, who opted to continue the work in Bradley's first person context, basing the remainder of the book on Blair's discussions and research involving Bradley's service and personal account.

Owens, Mackubin T. *U.S. Civil-Military Relations After 9/11: Renegotiating the Civil-Military Bargain.* New York: The Continuum International Publishing Group, 2011.

Owens provides a fresh look (2011) at the standard issues surrounding civil-military relations. Focusing on the post-9/11 context, he explores existing civil-military theories and their applicability given today's American societal values, as well as the role of the post-9/11 military and the type of military member that comprise it. Leveraging historical examples of civil-military dysfunction and taking into account the present security environment, Owens calls for a new civil-military "norm" that acknowledges the requirement for collaboration and the "overlapping and reciprocal interrelationships of ends ways and means necessary for strategic success."

Pearlman, Michael D. *Truman and MacArthur: Policy, Politics, and the Hunger for Honor and Renown.* Bloomington: Indiana University Press, 2008.

Truman and MacArthur is Pearlman's attempt to "fairly" dissect and present the facts surrounding Truman and MacArthur's relationship and interplay during the Korean War. By actively avoiding any perceived bias, his effort was to present a unique and accurate historical account that would not just be another "partisan polemic" that he labels others. Pearlman's in-depth and meticulous account indeed provides the political-military scholar with a unique perspective on the events surrounding the Korean War, as well as Truman and MacArthur's relationship. Pearlman admits that his work on this book shifted his previous misconceptions on the subject, and put him in a position to offer an "objective and comprehensive" point of view, which he believes is not skewed in support of, nor in opposition to, Truman or MacArthur's actions.

Perry, Mark. *Four Stars: The Inside Story of the Forty-Year Battle Between the Joint Chiefs of Staff and America's Civilian Leaders.* Boston: Houghton Mifflin, 1989.

Four Stars examines the relationship between the Joints Chiefs and civilian leadership surrounding the policy formulation and decision-making during the Cold War. His work focuses on, and examines civilian control at the highest echelon, describing the struggle between the military and civilian elite as both sides wrangle with advice and expertise into the formulation of U.S. policy.

Previdi, Robert. *Civilian Control Versus Military Rule.* New York: Hippocrene Books, 1988.

Drawing on 25 years of research and writings surrounding civil-military relations, Previdi examines the potential impact of the Goldwater-Nichols Act with respect to civilian control in America. Using the Korean War, The Cuban Missile Crisis and the Vietnam War as case studies and data points in civil-military relations, he illustrates why he believes the Goldwater-Nichols Act to be a "dangerous piece of legislation" that potentially skews the civil-military balance by granting the military too much power and influence. He concludes with a proposed reorganization that places the Secretary of Defense at the top, with both a military staff consisting of the service chiefs, and a civilian staff headed by civilian deputy secretaries of defense (both sharing the same organizational hierarchy), reporting collectively to the Secretary--a structure that he believes to be "the most efficient and effective way to manage the Department of Defense."

Priest, Dana. *The Mission: Waging War and Keeping Peace with America's Military*. New York: Norton, 2003.

Priest, a military correspondent for the Washington Post, examines what she believes to be the military's insidiously evolving role, which she contends has diverged from its conventional role and taken on greater responsibility and influence with respect to international affairs and policy--something she believes the military is ill-suited for and not prepared to successfully execute. Due to her direct access and her personal observations, she is able to leverage much of her first-hand information and provide gritty and detailed accounts surrounding senior military leader's personalities and actions (e.g., General Zinni). While her account provides a unique view of military responsibility and leadership playing out in an evolving and complex environment, it does not offer much in the way of scholarly analysis for the civil-military reader.

Rees, David. *Korea: The Limited War*. New York: St. Martin's Press, 1964

Rees, a British author, provides a detailed narrative of the Korean War that focuses largely on the political aspects that shaped the decisions and influenced civil-military relationships surrounding the Korean War. Rees also provides numerous appendices that detail force levels, units, commanders and historic documents.

Ridgway, Matthew B. *The Korean War*. Garden City: Doubleday, 1967.

This is General Ridgway's personal account surrounding his service in the Korean War. Succeeding General MacArthur as the U.N. Commander in Korea, General Ridgway was instrumental in rebuilding and reshaping a tattered force that had been beaten down by the North Korean and Chinese advance. The book highlights Ridgway's dealings and thoughts surrounding General MacArthur, as well as his successful strategy to push the North Koreans and Chinese back across the 38th parallel and achieve "victory." Ridgway also provides an analysis on the concept of "limited wars" and America's involvement in the containment of communism and the ensuing Cold War with the Soviets.

Snider, Don M., and Maranda A. Carlton-Carew. *U.S. Civil-Military Relations: In Crisis Or Transition?* Washington D.C.: The Center for Strategic and International Studies, 1995.

Another collection of essays centered on civil-military relations in the context of mid-1990s. Amid shrinking military budgets, limited resources, and shifting U.S. policy, the authors examine the state of civilian control and the overall relationship with the U.S. military. The authors examine the relevance of previous civil-military theories and thought, explore the impact of the evolving strategic landscape, and offer thought as to the future of civil-military relations.

Sorley, Lewis. *Honorable Warrior: General Harold Johnson and the Ethics of Command.* Lawrence: University Press of Kansas, 1998.

Honorable Warrior is a biography of General Johnson, who served as the Army Chief of Staff during the Vietnam War. The book details General Johnson's entire career, from his service during World War II, to his time as a field commander in Korea, through his service as the Army Chief of Staff. *Honorable Warrior* translates General Johnson's account of the discourse and mistrust surrounding the civil-military relationship during the Vietnam War--a unique and personal perspective from a key military leader.

Truman, Harry S. *Memoirs: Years of Trial and Hope.* Garden City: Doubleday, 1955.

Years of Trial on Hope is the follow-on (volume 2) to his first memoirs, *1945: Year of Decisions*, in which he details his decisions surrounding the use of the atomic bomb against the Japanese during World War II. *Years of Trial and Hope* serve as Truman's personal account of his key decisions and policy formulation from 1945 to 1952, chronicling not only his wartime leadership surrounding Korea and the Cold War with the Soviets, but on the domestic challenges and politics he faced concerning America.

Woodward, Bob. *Bush at War.* New York: Simon and Schuster, 2002.

A detailed account of President Bush's actions and decisions surrounding the 100 days following the terrorist attacks on 11 September 2001. Drawing from personal interviews with President Bush and other civilian and military leaders, Woodward paints a chronological picture exploring the highest-level decision-making processes and actions America took in the wake of the 9/11 attacks. The book provides great insight for the civil-military scholar researching the events leading up to U.S. action in Afghanistan.

-----. *Plan of Attack.* New York: Simon and Schuster, 2004.

Picking up where *Bush at War* left off, Woodward explores the leadership personalities and decision strategy that led to U.S. action in Iraq. Again, Woodward centers on the details of personalities, motivations and the key exchanges leading to war; critical for the civil-military scholar interested in researching U.S. strategic planning and war aims.

-----. *State of Denial: Bush at War.* New York: Simon and Shuster, 2006.

Drawing from *Bush at War and Plan of Attack, State of Denial* aims to uncover and illustrate the dysfunction among the civilian and military leaders that led to the continued U.S. involvement in Iraq. Because this book draws from Woodward's previous works surrounding the wars in Iraq and Afghanistan, *State of Denial* provides the civil-military reader with overarching lessons and analysis on both wars, as well as further detailed insight into the Bush Administration's formulation and execution of U.S. policy.

Academic Journals

Feaver, Peter D. "The Civil-Military Problematique: Huntington, Janowitz and the Question of Civilian Control." Armed Forces and Society 23, no. 2 (Winter 1996): 149-178.

Feaver examines the touchstone civil-military theories of Huntington and Janowitz within the context of the present-day military and the post-Cold War security requirements. He concludes that although Huntington and Janowitz were instrumental in crafting theories applicable in the Cold War era, the present-day environment calls for a new theory that distinctly defines and separates the civilian and military spheres, analyzes the factors that shape how civilians exercise control over the military, and finally, defines the concept and role that "military professionalism" plays in the current environment.

Johnson, David E. "Modern U.S. Civil-Military Relations: Wielding the Terrible Swift Sword." McNair Paper 57 (July 1997).

Johnson explores U.S. civil-military relations and policy formulation with respect to the Dayton Agreement and U.S. involvement in the Balkans. He argues that lessons drawn due to poor civil-military relations in Vietnam influenced civilian leaders into granting the military greater autonomy and influence into crafting U.S. defense policy in the mid-1990s. He concludes that in order to correct the "balance" of civilian control, civilian competencies must be emphasized by making political considerations paramount, and insist that military actions are tailored explicitly to meet

www.ingramcontent.com/pod-product-compliance
Lightning Source LLC
Chambersburg PA
CBHW052006280526
45793CB00005B/875